INTERNAT

ENERGY

DEVELOPMENT

SCOTT GAILLE

ISBN: 1466439475
ISBN 13: 9781466439474

To My Parents and Grandparents

"People will not look forward to posterity, who never look backward to their ancestors."

- Edmund Burke

TABLE OF CONTENTS

INTRODUCTION

This book is based on a class called International Energy Development that I have taught for several years to second-year MBA students at Rice University's Graduate School of Business. Although most of my Rice students are en route to positions in Houston's energy corridor, my course content assumes no prior energy experience. In fact, most of the principles taught in the course are generally applicable to international business development. Whether companies are pursuing international energy, timber, mining, or telecommunications concessions, many of the issues they face are similar to those we explore in class.

My Rice course is divided into two parts. The first half explores, from cradle to grave, how energy companies expand their businesses through international projects. The second half comprises case studies in upstream, midstream, and downstream energy projects from my own experiences, examining in detail different problems that were encountered in those projects and how they were addressed. The course concludes with a mock bidding round in which students participate as teams in an auction for exploration concessions in a West African nation. At the end of the auction, the teams have the opportunity to further diversify and adjust their petroleum portfolios through the purchase of other teams' concession interests. Finally, all of the teams participate in a drilling simulation and are able to see the creation (or destruction) of net present value.

This book focuses on the first half of my Rice course and begins with the project acquisition process I developed while working at Vinson & Elkins, Occidental Petroleum, and the Gaille Group. Following chapters discuss how international energy companies structure and operate international projects. Other topics include the emergence of national oil companies, approaches to the natural resources curse, and managing threats such as conflict and expropriation. My hope is that the reader of this book, like my students, will gain a new and better understanding of the challenges facing international energy development.

Scott Gaille
Houston, Texas – 2011

CHAPTER 1

THE BUSINESS DEVELOPMENT PROCESS

International energy transactions abound with complexity. Problems are magnified by the involvement of governments that play by unfamiliar rules—or sometimes by no rules at all. Obtaining information about international opportunities is challenging. Data may be incomplete or destroyed, and viewing it may require sending teams of personnel to the other side of the world, where they may face security and health risks. Negotiations may take considerably longer than anticipated and may be subject to misunderstandings as a result of varying cultures and styles of negotiation. Even after a contract is signed, renegotiation is common.

To mitigate international risks, it is important that business development be systematized. Over the course of my career as a lawyer and business development executive, I have settled on a process of seven steps that collectively enable a company to efficiently pursue and acquire the best international opportunities with aggressive risk management. The goal of these steps is to create a project pipeline in which the universe of projects is narrowed into a manageable subset, the economically attractive opportunities in the subset are identified, the available ones are found, negotiations are concluded, regulatory approvals are obtained, and risks are managed through portfolio economics.

GAILLE METHOD STEP ONE: IDENTIFY FOCUS AREA(S)

It is not possible for a company to evaluate every project in the world, and even the largest companies need to identify focus areas. This requires an honest appraisal of a company's strengths and weaknesses. What types of projects have been the most successful for the company? Why have they been successful? Because a company's expertise evolves over time, focus areas may take a variety of forms, some of which are planned while others are accidents of human capital or prior successes. For example, one of Occidental Petroleum's core businesses is acquiring assets that provide future growth through enhanced and improved oil recovery technology. Oxy also has geographic focus areas in California, the Permian Basin, Latin America, and the Middle East and tends to concentrate on oil rather than natural gas.

In terms of thinking about oil and gas focus areas, it is useful to characterize business concentrations as hydrocarbon-, reservoir-, life cycle-, or geography-based.

- *Hydrocarbon focus.* What type of hydrocarbon does the company wish to produce? Does the company prefer oil or natural gas? Oil prices tend to be determined by global markets whereas gas prices tend to be dictated by local market conditions. This is a consequence of the challenges and costs of transporting natural gas from low-demand to high-demand areas. Other focus areas might involve the quality characteristics of oil, such as lighter versus heavier crudes or high-sulfur versus low-sulfur crudes.

- *Reservoir focus.* This focus encompasses the development of conventional reservoirs (those capable of natural flow) and unconventional resources (those that require significant stimulation treatments or special recovery processes and technologies such as fracturing in shale production). Structural versus stratigraphic traps or clastics versus carbonates can also be areas of concentration.
- *Life cycle focus.* At what point in a project's life cycle does the company wish to enter—exploration, appraisal, development, early production, or mature production? In mature production, improved or enhanced oil recovery techniques, such as water and CO2 floods, can be further areas of specialization.
- *Geographic focus.* Where does the company wish to acquire the project? This concentration may involve regional focus, such as Africa versus the Middle East; or country focus, such as Nigeria versus Angola. Another consideration is offshore versus onshore. Offshore may be deep water or shallow water. Onshore could include a jungle or desert. Climatic focuses might include rough seas, arctic or arid conditions.

Adopting one or more of the above as focus areas enables a company to narrow the list of global projects down to a manageable size. One company might search the globe for unconventional shale capable of producing oil. Another might look at all types of projects in the Sultanate of Oman.

Within the focus area, the company must then decide how much capital it wishes to deploy and ask whether the expected expenditure is realistic in that focus area. These assumptions are usually tested with a focus area business plan. A focus area business plan starts with the assumption of a budget and then creates a hypothetical portfolio of assets using that budgeted amount. Proxy data regarding exploration, appraisal, development and operating costs, production profiles, and petroleum price curves can be obtained from the company's own records or industry sources. The focus area business plan typically includes a section on each hypothetical project that would be acquired, including its assumptions and economics (net present value and rate of return, among others).

The individual projects would then be fed into a focus area-wide section that would include assumptions about when each of the projects could be acquired and what overhead and business development costs would be incurred in the overall acquisition effort. This is also where sensitivities, such as indications of how the program's economics would be affected by changes in oil price or higher well costs, could come into play. Collectively, this information provides the business development executive with a scorecard showing how much value a successful acquisition program in a particular focus area would likely generate.

GAILLE METHOD STEP TWO:
USE TOP-DOWN EVALUATION TO CREATE A
TARGET LIST

Once a company has decided on a focus area, it should seek to identify the universe of projects that is available within that focus area. Step two involves a top-down analysis in which a company ignores the opportunities that are available for acquisition (i.e., for sale) and instead seeks to categorize and rank *all* of the focus area properties. To use the analogy of real estate, step one would represent the selection of a neighborhood in which a buyer is interested and in step two, the buyer would drive up and down the streets in the neighborhood to identify the best properties, irrespective of whether any houses are for sale at the time. Under step two of the Gaille Method, the business developer should catalog the opportunities in the focus area and then try to sort them based on attractiveness.

Although step two is a phase that companies sometimes skip, it creates efficiencies when it comes time to engage in steps three and four. For example, suppose there are ten projects available for purchase around the world in a particular focus area. A company that has fulfilled step two will already know which of these, if any, are best and will be able to focus its resources accordingly. The organization will not waste time undertaking expensive, bottom-up analyses of the low-ranking projects by sending technical teams to data rooms. Moreover, detailed analysis of the attractive projects should be more efficient because the company is already familiar with their value potential. This may enable the organization to move more quickly to a firm offer, thereby giving it a competitive advantage.

Step two also represents a form of active business development in which the company identifies projects it wants and then looks for buying opportunities *before* the potential properties are for sale. To the extent a company can identify where it wants to be, it can approach the current owners of those assets and make proactive overtures to acquire them. Even if the offers are rebuffed, the owners may change their minds at some point in the future and decide to sell. When they do, your company will be among the first that comes to mind. This approach may position your company to buy an asset before it is ever placed on the market. Even if some of your competitors are following the same active strategy, it will at least put you on a short list of potential buyers, whereas a company that simply waits for projects to go on sale might never have the opportunity to participate.

The top-down process of evaluating the universe of projects can produce unique and valuable information about hidden potential and risks in a focus area. This results primarily from identifying analogues of success and failure. In other words, a top-down comparative analysis will provide a company with a greater understanding of what characteristics have led to varying degrees of success and failure in a focus area and should help it to select better projects. Similarly, a global perspective can help in the identification of trends and enable a company to see how an approach or idea in one project might be duplicated or extended in another. In contrast, simply evaluating projects on a one-by-one basis may not provide enough points of comparison to achieve the connections that often result from a methodical, top-down analysis.

Let's look at an example of how the top-down process might work. If the focus area were Sub-Saharan African exploration, the company would compile a list of the approximately eighteen hundred petroleum blocks that are spread throughout the countries of Sub-Saharan Africa. It would then set out to gather seismic data, well reports, and other analyses on as many of these blocks as possible. Comparative analysis would then be carried out in which geologic teams would seek to identify structures capable of holding large amounts of petroleum as well as trends of existing discoveries and dry holes. The result of this process might be a list of about one hundred high-potential target blocks that are favorably comparable to exploration successes elsewhere and that have reservoir potential capable of holding commercial amounts of petroleum. Perhaps one thousand of these blocks might be excluded as being unattractive because of their higher risk of failure for one reason or another, and the remainder might stay on a "maybe" or "watch" list, from which they may be elevated or demoted as a result of the success or failure of future wells.

At the end of the top-down process, the company should have identified a subset of opportunities that are particularly attractive (or at least eliminated a subset that are unattractive). Step two provides the company with a broad vision of the opportunities in the focus area and enables it to carry out its acquisition process with the knowledge of which projects are, relatively speaking, better than others, given all of the available data.

GAILLE METHOD STEP THREE:
ACCESS PROJECTS ON THE TARGET LIST

It is often the case that a company's business development efforts amount to little more than tracking which assets are being sold by which companies and then attending data rooms to evaluate these assets. In contrast, the Gaille Method suggests an active approach to business development in which the company uses the target list compiled in step two to pursue the projects it views as most attractive, irrespective of whether they are for sale.

The starting point for step three is identifying owners of targeted assets and the executives responsible for managing them. The company should contact each of the executives and request a meeting. At this meeting, your organization can explain its focus area and express interest in acquiring a position in the asset(s). Even if the owner declines your overture, the knowledge that there is a willing, interested buyer (who might pay a premium price) could result in the owner reconsidering at a later date.

A company seeking to acquire assets should remember that a proactive approach facilitates deals because it decreases the *transactions* costs of selling an asset. If a company has a readily available buyer for an asset, it may enable the organization to skip a burdensome sales process. The usual one requires a seller to prepare a data room and answer questions from prospective buyers. This "open house" approach to selling assets consumes considerable time and resources. The seller may also find that it needs to enlist the help of an investment bank to market the asset, which entails additional fees.

It also is important to contact each of the governments where targeted assets are located. U.S. embassies in individual countries will assist in setting up meetings and arranging for interpreters, if necessary. The company should send a senior executive with international experience to each nation to meet with the oil minister, the head of the national oil company (if one exists), and perhaps representatives of the finance ministry or head of state's office. During these meetings, the executive should provide the background of your company and its expertise and then share the organization's focus areas, including the specific project(s) in the host country that are of interest and why.

Often, the government holds contractual interests in a petroleum project. These include (a) carried interests, where one or more companies pay some or all of the costs allocable to the government interest but where the government is entitled to a share of the petroleum, and (b) back-in rights, where the government has the option to acquire a participating interest in the project at some point in the future, typically upon paying its pro rata share of costs. A government may even sell some of its royalty or production-sharing entitlement based on discounted cash flow economics. If your company believes that the project has more upside than the government assumes, it might be able to buy these interests at an attractive price.

Even if no deal can be reached with the government, establishing a relationship and expressing interest in a specific project can improve your organization's chances of success down the road. For example, the government may alert you of plans by a project owner to sell. Or, better yet, the government could make use of its preferential purchase rights to steer a transaction to your company's doorstep. In most international energy projects, the government has the right to approve the buyer of any interest. If the government likes your company, it may encourage the owner to sell the asset to you. In these situations, the government will typically become a middleman and exercise its preferential purchase right at price x and then offer to sell to your company at a premium price of $x + y$. Depending on the value your organization sees in the project, paying a premium to participate and eliminate competitors may be reasonable.

Using the example of Sub-Saharan African exploration blocks, assume that one hundred blocks were identified on the target list and that these blocks were scattered over twelve nations and owned by sixty different companies. Some blocks have multiple owners. Some owners have positions in several of these blocks. Step three of the process would be to meet with the governments of the nations where there are the most blocks on your short list (the most likely places where acquisitions will take place) and with the companies who own the most block interests. In both cases, it may be possible to achieve a "package deal" where a government or owner enables your company to acquire interests in multiple assets as part of a single deal. It is not uncommon for companies to change focus areas and entirely divest a portfolio of assets. If several assets in a divestment portfolio are on your organization's target list, you might opt to acquire the whole package and then later shed those assets viewed as less attractive. As step three progresses, it will spin off acquisition opportunities, which will be addressed in step four. A company may progress through the list of governments and companies pursuant to step three even as initial assets are being acquired in latter stages of the Gaille Method.

GAILLE METHOD STEP FOUR:
CONDUCT A BOTTOM-UP EVALUATION OF
ACCESSIBLE PROJECTS

Step four in the Gaille Method represents a detailed, bottom-up evaluation of an energy opportunity. Knowing that an opportunity is among the top 5 or 10 percent of those surveyed in a top-down analysis helps a great deal, but due to confidentiality of data, it is rare that your company will ever see all of the available information about an opportunity during its preliminary analysis. Due diligence requires a more detailed inspection to confirm your company's initial expectations.

Before this evaluation begins, the prospective buyer and seller will enter into an agreement typically called a confidentiality agreement (CA) or nondisclosure agreement (NDA). This document will require that the potential buyer keep any information he or she receives strictly confidential and only use it for an evaluation of the potential acquisition. Once this document is signed, the project review can begin in earnest.

A business development executive acts much like an air-traffic controller at this point, directing various lawyers, geologists, geophysicists, drillers, engineers, and economists through the evaluation of the asset. The buyer's U.S.-based legal counsel will review all contracts related to the project and will be supported by a local counsel in the host nation, who will at least confirm that the current owner has good, legal title to the asset. The lawyers will also identify any approvals that may be required before the transaction can close. Together with the attorneys, the business developer will arrive at certain assumptions regarding legal and commercial terms such as taxes, royalties, and production sharing based on the laws of the host nation and the applicable contracts. Similarly, the technical team will review the geology, geophysics, reservoir, wells, and engineering of the opportunity and provide forecasts for costs, production, and reserves under various risk scenarios. All of this information will be analyzed by an economist, who will construct an economic model to determine how much money the company can expect to make (or lose) under various assumptions. The goal of this model is to show the value of the acquisition under different scenarios, which are usually assigned probabilities of occurrence.

Your company needs to be wary of the assumptions that go into the economic model. Self-preservation can taint recommendations if the acquisition of a project means employment of a team member for many years during the project's development phase. Further, assumptions can be unduly influenced by one or more individuals or even by the group's impression of what they think the company wants to hear. A project that was on the target list from step two or is otherwise part of a focus area where the company wishes to grow tends to be viewed more favorably, and assumptions could be skewed to validate the mission of your company.

In order to mitigate this risk, a process of independent voting can be implemented before technical team members meet to discuss the assumptions going into the project's economic model. The use of independent voting in various contexts has been the subject of numerous articles and books, including James Surowiecki's *Wisdom of Crowds*. One of the best-known examples of independent voting is the estimation of a volume, such as the number of jelly beans in a jar. In this example, a jar containing thousands of jelly beans is placed in a public place and individuals are allowed to guess how many jelly beans are in the jar, with the closest one winning a prize. This experiment has shown that, with enough independent guesses, the average of the independent votes is usually within a few percentage points of the actual number and may even be closer than the best individual estimate. Having geologists predict how many barrels of oil are in a reservoir is not that different from guessing how many jelly beans are in a jar.

In its purest form, the company will undertake this voting process by requiring each technical person to submit his or her numbers on key metrics in a manner similar to a secret ballot. In this way, the company can obtain the unfiltered, independent views of each individual without any concern that they may be judged negatively if their views are out of step with the company. If this is not practical, another alternative is for the business development executive to walk the halls prior to the first meeting and visit privately with each technical person, informally recording each individual's views. However obtained, the numbers should be aggregated to arrive at an independent average of each important assumption in the economic model.

Typically, the technical team will gather in a risk-assessment meeting to arrive at their collective assumptions through a deliberative process where they may debate alternative views and try to arrive at a consensus. This "team" number can then be compared to the "independent" voting average. In my experience, the team numbers tend to be higher than the independent average when the company is in an acquisition posture and lower than the independent average when the company is reconsidering an existing project or is in an exit posture. Thus, a business development executive undertaking an acquisition program should probably be wary of any project that just barely meets the company's economic thresholds and should instead look for a comfortable premium to protect against overly enthusiastic assumptions.

There are several other data points of value that can be obtained by comparing the consensus assumptions with the independent voting results:

- *The range between the team number and the independent voting average.* The greater this range, the greater the concern for a flaw in the consensus evaluation. Has a minority opinion prevailed? Has one individual imposed his views on the group?
- *The range of the independent votes.* The narrower the range of independent votes, the less risky the project is because the independent views of several people are not that far

apart. If the most pessimistic person is right, the project's economics may still be fine. Conversely, if someone views the opportunity highly negatively, this may be cause for concern.
- *The distribution of independent votes.* If the views of the technical team are spread randomly over a range, it likely reflects a general uncertainty. If the votes are concentrated around a couple of different positions, it probably reflects a difference of view on a key assumption. In this case, the business development executive may need to understand what technical sensitivity the team members disagree on.

The goal of step four in the Gaille Method is to undertake a bottom-up analysis of an opportunity that (a) is within the focus area identified in step one, (b) is among those opportunities that were short-listed in the top-down analysis in step two, and (c) has a willing seller as identified in step three. By funneling opportunities in this way, the considerable resources required in a rigorous bottom-up analysis are focused on a small handful of projects that the company is interested in acquiring and that the owners are willing to sell. This avoids wasted evaluations and enables the company to conduct more rigorous due diligence on a smaller number of projects.

GAILLE METHOD STEP FIVE:
NEGOTIATE TRANSACTIONS

Once the company has completed a bottom-up analysis, the process of negotiation can begin. Negotiation usually starts with the principal commercial terms, most notably price. This may occur in person or via written correspondence in which companies exchange letters of offer and counteroffer, gradually narrowing their range of difference. If the companies can reach agreement on the principal commercial terms, they are usually committed to a short document that may be called a letter of intent (LOI), a memorandum or understanding (MOU), or a heads of agreement (HOA).

Should the LOI, MOU, or HOA be legally binding at this stage? If, for some reason, the parties do not proceed further, is there enough detail in the LOI, MOU, or HOA for an arbitrator to enforce it? Practically speaking, the fewer open commercial terms at this stage, the greater the likelihood that the parties will be comfortable making the preliminary document legally binding.

As a general rule, it is in the acquiring company's interest to lock in the seller through a binding document as quickly as possible. Otherwise, there is a risk that your nonbinding document or even verbal discussions—which essentially constitute an indicative and unaccepted offer—could be shopped to others. Once one company has undertaken the expense and work to evaluate a project and make a firm offer, a second organization may be able to free ride on the first company's initial work and thereby easily offer a little bit more.

For this same reason, the acquiring company will generally wish to advance the pace of the transaction as quickly as possible. The appearance of a rival bidder at any stage before closing could cause the seller to look for ways to get out of its deal with your organization so that it can sell at a higher price. That being said, some jurisdictions, such as Texas, provide protections to prospective relationships and contracts through the law of tortuous interference, which prohibits third parties from disrupting such relationships under certain circumstances.

A binding LOI, MOU, or HOA with specificity of commercial terms may have other tangential benefits. It may enable a company to start its own internal approval process, such as obtaining the approval of the board of directors. Depending on the organization, this can be a time-consuming process and it is best to get it underway in conjunction with the drafting and negotiation of the definitive documents. In the case of material transactions, such a document may also help a company manage its public disclosure requirements by decreasing the period of limbo during which insiders might trade its stock before the definitive agreement is announced to the public.

Whether or not the preliminary document is binding, the definitive documents should be consistent with its terms unless the parties mutually agree otherwise. Depending on how the transaction is to be structured, the long-form document is usually either a variation of a stock purchase and sale agreement, whereby the acquiring company takes ownership of the stock of a special purpose entity that usually owns nothing other than the project, or an asset purchase and sale agreement, whereby the asset is conveyed. As will be discussed later in this book, most international assets are held through special purpose entities that provide the company with a variety of advantages, including the flexibility to sell the asset indirectly through the sale of a company that owns nothing else. Which direction is elected may be affected by, among other things, U.S. tax or local tax considerations and whether the preferential purchase rights of the host government or other companies apply equally to stock and asset transactions.

One consideration to keep in mind is that the time line for negotiating international transactions increases if one of the parties is from a different nation or is a government. A negotiation between two large American companies familiar with one another might take less than two months from the time of the letter of intent to the final approval of the board of directors, whereas a negotiation with a foreign government could easily take more than six months. One reason for this is that government negotiators may not have the authority to compromise during negotiation sessions, which may result in many deferred items from negotiation session to session. These open items will then have to be brought back to the attention of the oil minister or others for deliberation before another meeting can be scheduled.

The length of the negotiation process can be shortened by your company's approach to negotiations. In particular, taking consistent, middle-of-the-road positions on contentious issues can encourage the other party to do the same and can expedite the negotiation process. The energy industry is a remarkably small world, and you and your organization are likely to see the same parties on different sides of transactions. Inconsistency or gamesmanship on issues will be noticed and leads to mistrust and a general slowing of the process. When Chevron is selling to your company this month and buying from your company next month, the assumption of inconsistent positions with Chevron is likely to create problems.

Many companies try to adopt standard positions and form agreements for repeating transactions. These documents seek to take middle-of-the-road positions (and legal language) so that the company can accept the same positions and language on many issues regardless of whether it is the buyer or seller in a transaction. This enables an organization to commence the negotiation by stating that the position or language being proposed is the same as your company would accept on the other side of the table. Such consistency can defuse conflict and help to swiftly move the documents to signature.

Above all, remember that time is often the enemy. If your company is keen to buy or sell and has found a willing counterparty at a price it views as attractive, then by all means move as quickly as you can to complete negotiations and execute the definitive documents. The more time that passes during a negotiation, the greater the risk that some event will overtake your transaction and derail it. To minimize this risk, any negotiation tactic that is likely to prolong the course of negotiations should generally be avoided.

GAILLE METHOD STEP SIX:
OBTAIN APPROVALS AND COUNTRY ENTRY

Transactions in the United States may be subject to third-party approvals, such as from partners, or to preferential purchase rights. Third-party approvals are common in international transactions, too. Even after signing definitive documents, the seller may be obligated to offer your deal to one of its partners, and if such party accepts on the same terms, your company will lose the transaction after investing considerable time and cost in its pursuit, evaluation, and negotiation.

Where international transactions become more complex is in the extent to which the host government may become involved. The host government may have its own preferential purchase right, which is more dangerous than one held by a company partner.

A government may exercise this right, or threaten to exercise it, and then proceed to market the terms and conditions of your company's transaction to other potential buyers in pursuit of a higher price. If the government can obtain a higher price, it will then be able to flip the asset to a new buyer and pocket the difference between the cost of acquiring the asset on the terms and conditions negotiated by your organization and whatever price it was able to obtain elsewhere. A government may even have special relationships with other companies that it wishes to further by channeling projects to them. For example, one government may court the favor of another nation by steering projects to its oil companies. If a government has a preferential purchase right, it will be important for your company to visit with the oil minister during the negotiation process to try to better understand the government's intentions. If you cultivate this relationship, the government may give your organization the final opportunity to price match.

Even in the absence of preferential purchase rights, the government invariably has assignment approval rights of one kind or another. These rights are legally drafted in various ways: sometimes they are discretionary, but more commonly they are constrained by language such as "not to be unreasonably withheld or delayed" or with the requirement that the government approve any assignment if the buyer is technically and financially capable. The practical matter is that your company cannot obtain clean title to the asset without the host government's approval. If the government withholds its approval, whether it is allowed to or not, the problems created through clouding the title are usually so great that the transaction is canceled. The one exception to this applies to nonoperated interests where the seller can sometimes remain the owner of record opposite the government but the buyer takes all of the risks and rewards for the interest through a private trust arrangement.

If your company follows the Gaille Method, by this point it has already visited the oil minister and other key officials in the government at least once and has previously telegraphed its intention to acquire assets in the host country, including the specific asset at hand. As soon as the transaction becomes binding, both the buyer and seller should jointly travel in person to meet with the oil minister to describe the transaction and respectfully request his or her support for its conclusion. Both parties should be careful to recognize the sovereignty of the government and should not imply that the government's review and approval of the transaction is perfunctory or assumed. Approval should be humbly and respectfully requested.

When dealing with foreign governments, there are often multiple sets of approvals required. There is usually a formal process delineated in the petroleum law, which may include the approval of the oil minister, the national oil company, a presidential or council of minister's decree, or even an act of legislation. Parallel to this, there may be an informal process whereby one or more advisors to these entities participate in the decision. If there is an informal process, it is important that your company follows it. The selling company or your local counsel will make you aware of such requirements.

Finally, there may be a whole host of other approvals relating to your company establishing a business presence in the foreign country, which are independent and above and beyond anything related to the petroleum approval process. These might include

- Incorporation of a local entity
- Business permit
- Tax permit

One African country has a ten-step approval process for a business permit. This laborious effort requires representatives of the applicant to visit periodically to ascertain whether the company's paperwork has progressed upward through six different desks, starting with the Schedule Officer of the Citizens and Business Department and ending with the Minister of Internal Affairs, with each desk needing to stamp its approval. Once the Minister's approval has been attained, the documents then return, in reverse order back through the desks so that each of the parties can note that the Minister has approved the application.

While a later chapter discusses the problem of corruption, the Foreign Corrupt Practices Act makes it a crime for U.S. companies or citizens to offer bribes to foreign officials. From time to time, foreign officials may seek to be illegally compensated by requesting payment from companies pursuing their government's approval. Such behavior is usually also illegal in the host country and can result in the local prosecution of the government official and individuals from your organization. Violating such laws may lead to the invalidation of the transaction and your company losing the right to do business there. For these reasons, it is essential that your organization rigorously enforce ethical business conduct to ensure that such laws are not violated.

GAILLE METHOD STEP SEVEN: CONSTRUCT A PORTFOLIO

The last step of the Gaille Method constitutes an additional level of risk management. However thorough your top-down and bottom-up analyses are, circumstances beyond the reasonable control of the company can impact a project. Countries can descend into civil war. Sanctions can be imposed that prevent U.S. companies from doing business in certain regions. Projects can fail for a variety of reasons that were not foreseeable at the outset.

When one project has been acquired and subsequent ventures are being evaluated, it is important to consider how each additional project impacts the collective risk of the portfolio.

- *Country risk.* Having projects in multiple *countries* helps to insulate the cash flow of the organization from country-specific events, whether political or natural. For example, if there are three attractive projects available in one country, your company may decline two of these and instead wait for projects to become available in other regions.
- *Project risk.* Having investments in multiple *projects* helps to protect the cash flow of the organization from project-specific events such as higher capital or operating costs, lower revenues, or technical errors. For example, even though your company might be able to acquire 50 percent

of a particular project, it might opt for 25 percent of that project and 25 percent of another in order to minimize the concentration of capital in any one project.

- *Exploration risk.* Another type of risk that can be mitigated in this way is *exploration* risk. A company could spend $120 million on one exploration well with a 30 percent chance of success or $120 million on six one-fifth interests in six different exploration wells, each with a 30 percent chance of success. The chance of losing the $120 million investment in the concentrated case is 70 percent (the probability of one dry hole), whereas the chance of losing the entire investment in the six-well program is about 12 percent (the probability that all six wells will be dry). Most companies would prefer the diversified case, where there is an 88 percent chance that one of the wells will be successful—even if the returns will be smaller.

- *Sequential risk.* Having investments in projects that are uncorrelated or at least less correlated is important. For example, during the acquisition of petroleum blocks, a company should ask whether the failure of an exploration well on any of its existing blocks would increase the chance of failure on the new block. Your organization may want to avoid projects that are sequentially linked in this way because they can multiply the amount of capital risked by a single unfavorable event or outcome.

- *Diversity of experience.* Participating in varied projects in different countries provides exposure to a wide range of business approaches and solutions within your focus area, which creates the opportunity to apply lessons learned in one project to others.

THE GAILLE METHOD SUMMARIZED

The Gaille Method for international energy development is a methodical process that encompasses seven steps:

(1) *Identify focus area(s).* A company should ascertain its strengths and apply them to focus areas in which it has a competitive advantage and in which the universe of possible transactions is manageable for the organization to evaluate.

(2) *Use top-down evaluation to create a target list.* Within each focus area, a company should create a list of all available opportunities and then sort those in a way that results in a target list of the most attractive ones—that is, those projects that the organization would be most interested in joining.

(3) *Access projects on the target list.* Once a target list has been identified, the organization should ascertain who owns interests in the targeted projects and approach the companies and governments involved in order to identify which of the projects can be acquired.

(4) *Conduct a bottom-up evaluation of accessible opportunities.* Once the company has identified which of its target list projects are for sale, it should engage in a rigorous due diligence to confirm that each available project is as attractive as originally thought.

(5) *Negotiate transactions.* Assuming that the project passes due diligence tests, the company should move as quickly as possible to conclude one or more binding agreements to secure the transaction.

(6) *Obtain approvals and country entry.* The government approval process can be among the most difficult aspects of an international transaction. The organization will need to carefully manage its relationship with the host government if it wishes to close the deal.

(7) *Construct a portfolio.* As a company moves to acquire multiple projects in its focus area, it is important to consider how the projects being acquired impact different risks. This portfolio overlay could cause a company to decline projects that might otherwise meet its criteria.

CHAPTER 2

PRELIMINARY AGREEMENTS

D uring the pre-acquisition phase of business development, companies may enter into various contractual arrangements that facilitate the evaluation or sale of interests among them. These include

- *Confidentiality Agreement/Nondisclosure Agreement.* The CA and NDA make possible the disclosure of confidential information from a seller to a prospective buyer.
- *Joint Study and Bidding Agreement (JSBA).* Under this agreement, two or more companies collaborate in the evaluation of a project and discuss what type of offer they might make and how any successful acquisition would be divided among them and operated.
- *Area of Mutual Interest (AMI) Agreement.* The AMI Agreement is a version of the JSBA in which one or more companies do not collaborate in the pursuit of projects, but agree to share any projects they may acquire in accordance with its terms.

- *Joint Marketing and Sale Agreement.* This type of arrangement enables two or more owners of the same asset to divest a part of the asset on a pro rata basis and to share the costs of marketing that asset.

CONFIDENTIALITY/NONDISCLOSURE AGREEMENT

Before a company commences any detailed discussions with a third party, it should enter into an agreement that provides for confidentiality. These agreements can be structured so that they are one-way, with only one disclosing party and one receiving party, or two-way, in which both parties to the agreement simultaneously disclose and receive confidential information. The principal provisions are as follows:

- *Scope.* The more precisely defined the scope of the confidentiality agreement, the better. For example, in the context of a petroleum exploration block, the confidentiality agreement typically provides the country and block name and refers to a map attached as an annex, which shows the geographical limits of the area being discussed.
- *Nondisclosure undertaking.* The agreement provides that, as a general rule, information within its scope is confidential and the receiving party may not disclose it to others.
- *Exclusions to confidentiality.* Whether styled as exceptions to the undertaking or exclusions from the definition of confidential information, these agreements do not restrict information that is already known to the recipient, is already public or becomes public without the recipient's involvement, or is acquired or developed independently.
- *Permitted disclosures on a need–to-know basis.* The confidentiality agreement permits disclosures to employees, officers, and directors of the receiving party and its affiliates, consultants, counsel, and financing agents provided that the agreement's provisions extend to such individuals.

- *Permitted use of information.* The confidential information shall only be used for specific purposes, such as to allow the recipient to evaluate whether to enter into a transaction with the disclosing party.
- *Warranty of disclosing party.* The disclosing party warrants that it has the right and authority to disclose the information to the receiving party.
- *Return/destruction.* The disclosed information must generally be returned or destroyed within a period of time after the evaluation ends.
- *Term and termination.* The term of the agreement may be a subject of contention, as the disclosing party will want it to be longer than the receiving party. Terms are usually on the order of one to five years.

JOINT STUDY AND BIDDING AGREEMENT

Joint Study and Bidding Agreements are arrangements in which two or more companies collaborate on a particular focus area. These companies pool their resources in various ways through the sharing of data, expertise, personnel, and capital. If their efforts result in assets being acquired, the companies have to decide how those assets are to be shared. They must also select an operator.

Such collaborations often arise when a country holds an auction, or bidding round, in which government-owned energy assets are offered to the public. Dozens of different companies may be interested in the assets being auctioned and there can be a period when these companies partner with one another to form consortia. This can be disadvantageous to the government, though, as it results in fewer independent bids. Sometimes, the government's rules of bidding prohibit consortia and require all bids to be placed by individual parties.

Bid rounds are often utilized for the most attractive petroleum exploration acreages in countries such as Nigeria, Angola, and Libya. Figure 2.1 below illustrates how the Government of Angola has divided its territory into blocks of varying sizes that different companies have acquired in the past or may bid for in the future. Participation in these auction exercises is highly uncertain and exposes bidding companies to substantial risk. At the outset, there may be dozens of petroleum blocks being placed up for auction. It requires considerable resources to evaluate and understand the opportunities well enough to place a bid. The probability that such costs will be incurred without gaining a license is high because of the competitive bidding. By sharing and pooling resources with other companies, the cost of preparation (and of losing) can be somewhat diminished.

Figure 2.1: Map of Petroleum Blocks in Angola

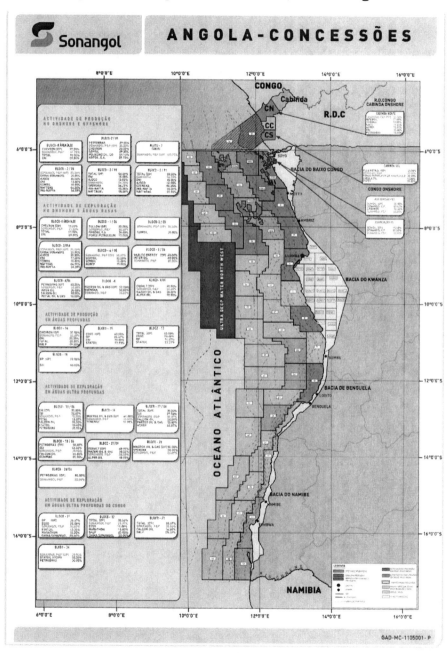

On one hand, there are economies of scale involved in evaluating all of the blocks, and some companies may bid on most of them with the expectation that it may take many bids to win one or two blocks. On the other, there is always the risk that a bidder will win all of its bids and find that it has acquired obligations far in excess of what it expected. Bidding rules may require the placement of simultaneous bids, each of which is binding on the company that places it. Consortia help to mitigate this risk because the companies involved agree to divide each asset between them, thereby decreasing the capital exposure if several bids are successful.

These arrangements can also be used outside the bidding round context. For example, companies might form a consortium to evaluate worldwide ultra-deepwater exploration opportunities and undertake a business development process such as the Gaille Method. This might enable two smaller companies to better manage the costs of a top-down analysis of all the opportunities in a larger focus area.

The principal provisions of a Joint Study and Bidding Agreement are as follows:

- *Definition of area.* The study or bidding area must be carefully defined to avoid ambiguity concerning what the companies are working on together and what obligations of sharing those companies have with one another. Ambiguities can lead to disputes if one company independently secures an opportunity that another company in the JSBA thought was covered by the scope of the JSBA. Precision is easier if the area can be defined geographically—by a map or by blocks. If the joint study area is a global study of a certain kind of opportunity or only includes certain types of opportunities in a geographic area, for example, the definition of the area can become challenging. The more layers of complexity included in the definition of the area, the greater the likelihood of dispute over whether some future project is covered by the definition.
- *Structure of cooperation.* How will the parties work together? Will there be a division of labor such that one company

analyzes half of the opportunities and the second analyzes the other half (and they come together at a later date to share their conclusions)? Will each company contribute personnel to analyze all of the projects together in joint meetings? Or will each of the companies analyze all of the projects separately and then meet at the conclusion of the process to share their views and arrive at a consensus about which projects they should pursue?

- *Study cost participation.* How are costs of the joint study being shared among the parties? The usual process is for each company to bear its own costs of the technical study, although this poses the risk that one company will bring more of its personnel and resources to bear on the work. If one company incurs a disproportionate share of the work, there will likely be a cost equalization provision.

- *Decision process.* A process should be established by which the members of the consortium will vote on which projects to pursue. Practically speaking, the more companies involved in such a process, the greater the likelihood that one company will not want to participate in one or more projects. The JSBA contains provisions for enabling the parties to vote on whether they will move forward and on what terms. Typically, parties that vote against a project are not required to participate, but the remaining party(ies) are able to continue with the acquisition without having further obligation to share that project with those opting out.

- *Project participation.* If the consortium secures one or more assets, how will those assets be divided? What will be the participating interest of each company in each project? Assuming that all parties begin from a roughly level playing field, the typical approach is pro rata participation in the projects, with each party paying its share of the costs and receiving the same share of petroleum and revenues. That being said, the division of participating interest is a commercial term that reflects the financial and technical strengths of the parties and whether one or more of the parties has already advanced the work in the focus area.

This can lead to different percentages of participation or to situations in which one party pays a higher percentage of the costs than it will receive in revenues (referred to as "carrying" the other party(ies)).

- *Operatorship.* Most international projects require the naming of a single operator company that will manage the project. Operatorship is discussed in more detail later in the book, but the JSBA will need to have a mechanism for its allocation. Will one company always operate? Will the companies alternate such that the first project operatorship goes to company A, the second project's operatorship goes to company B, and so on? Will the organizations create a joint venture company to which they will each loan employees?

- *Termination.* JSBAs must include carefully crafted termination provisions that enable the parties to terminate the arrangement and that specify how jointly developed data is handled after the termination. Usually, there is a long-stop date, after which the parties are no longer required to pursue projects together or otherwise share interests. At that point, any projects they acquired together continue on their own terms, each party gets a copy of the jointly developed data, and the parties are then free to pursue future projects independently.

Area of Mutual Interest Agreement

An Area of Mutual Interest Agreement in many respects resembles a JSBA, although AMI Agreements merely require the parties to share projects that they may independently acquire in a focus area. Such arrangements generally do not entail any cooperation with respect to the evaluation or pursuit of opportunities. The only time the counterparty even learns about an opportunity is after the other party has acquired it, at which point the offering party must provide the other with the option to buy an interest in the new project on such terms and conditions as agreed in the AMI.

The principal provisions of an AMI Agreement are as follows:

- *Definition of area.* The definition of area in the AMI Agreement raises similar issues as the JSBA, but an AMI may be more geographically defined since it is a results-oriented agreement.
- *Participation right.* What level of participation is each party entitled to in the counterparty's projects? The participation of the offering party is often much higher, typically two-to-one. This is because the party that identifies, pursues, and secures the project should be rewarded, which provides an incentive for acquiring more projects.
- *Option process.* The key procedure defined in the AMI Agreement is how the parties offer participation in projects to others. There are time lines for how long after closing a project the offering party must provide the receiving party access to data regarding the project and how long the receiving party has to evaluate the project before providing notice of its intent to participate.
- *Cost of participation.* As a general rule, AMI participation is on a ground-floor basis, such that the receiving party pays its pro rata share of the costs (historical and future). There can be variations around this point, though, as AMIs may require the receiving party to pay, for example, 150 percent of the historic costs. AMIs also may grant the recipient a small net profits interest or royalty right in projects that are acquired by the other company. In these circumstances, the cost of participation is effectively zero and there is usually no option process. Such arrangements may reward one company for introducing another to the area.

JOINT MARKETING AND SALE AGREEMENT

The Joint Marketing and Sale Agreement arises when more than one company owns a single asset and *multiple* owners are interested in divestment. Rather than competing against each other and having duplicate data rooms, companies typically cooperate. In order to do so, they need an agreement that sets forth how they will allocate costs, manage offers, and share in the rights and obligations of any sales contract that results.

- *Structure of cooperation.* Many of the issues with the JSBA are present in a context in which two parties are jointly marketing their separate interests in an energy project. How will the parties work together? Will there be a division of labor such that one company contacts certain prospective buyers and the second company contacts the remainder? Will one company provide the data room for prospective buyers to review the project or will each company host an identical data room and allow prospective buyers to attend either location? This might be advantageous if, for example, one company is located in Houston and the other in London. Will the companies hire a third party such as an investment bank to create an electronic data room and conduct the joint marketing on their behalf?
- *Cost participation.* How are costs of the marketing and data room to be allocated and shared among the parties? The usual process is for each company to bear its own internal costs; external costs, such as investment banking costs, are divided among them in accordance with the ratio of interests they are seeking to sell. For example, if party A owns two-thirds of the project and party B owns one-third, and each are trying to divest their entire interests, third-party costs would be shared on a two-thirds to one-third basis.
- *Decision process.* A process should be established by which involved parties either accept or reject offers. If an offer is received and both companies wish to accept it, then they both enter into sales and purchase agreements with the buyer on the same terms and conditions. In the event that only one seller accepts the offer, it needs to be able to conclude the sale on its own.
- *Partial sales.* If an offer is received for less than all of the interest that is for sale, the agreement should contain a

mechanism whereby each party can sell part of its interest on a pro rata basis. For example, if a buyer offers to acquire 50 percent of an asset held currently by party A at two-thirds and party B at one-third, each would sell half of its interest (party A would sell a 33 percent interest and party B would sell a 17 percent interest).

CONCLUSION

During the process of evaluating, pursuing, and marketing assets, a business developer will enter into a variety of preliminary contractual arrangements. Confidentiality and Nondisclosure Agreements are ubiquitous in the industry and are a prerequisite to the disclosure of confidential information to prospective buyers. During the pursuit of projects, companies also may cooperate and share the costs and rewards. The Joint Study and Bidding Agreement enables organizations to jointly evaluate opportunities and arrive at offers. When their efforts result in an acquisition, the JSBA sets forth how the project's ownership will be divided and which company will operate. The Area of Mutual Interest Agreement is a variation on the JSBA pursuant to which companies separately pursue projects, but the acquiring company still assigns a participating interest to the other. When it comes time to divest a project, companies may similarly cooperate through a Joint Marketing and Sale Agreement, which enables two or more sellers of the same asset to share marketing costs.

CHAPTER 3

PROJECT EVALUATIONS

O ur discussion of the Gaille Method introduced various approaches to evaluating projects that involve categorizing them as part of either a top-down process or a bottom-up process. The top-down analysis adds considerable value in terms of informing a company about which projects within a focus area look the most attractive on a cursory examination. A more detailed bottom-up evaluation is needed to properly test each project to confirm that it meets the company's technical, legal, and economic standards. Both are important to ensuring that a company acquires quality projects that are consistent with its acquisition criteria.

TOP-DOWN AND BOTTOM-UP ANALYSIS

The top-down analysis is a *comparative* one through which the projects within a focus area are weighed against one another. This process looks at how the attributes of different projects are similar (or dissimilar) to analogues of success and failure within a focus area. The practical result of top-down comparative analysis is that a company is able to rank the projects in a focus area to determine which projects it would like to pursue. The top-down process starts with every prospect in the focus area and funnels them into a more manageable handful of the best opportunities.

The value of a comparative analysis is significant. For example, in the context of petroleum exploration, the relative potential of petroleum blocks can be ranked through technical criteria. How many prospects exist on a block? How large are those prospects? What is the likelihood that those prospects will contain petroleum? How do the prospects compare to analogues of success? How do they compare to analogues of failure? Comparative analysis provides an indication of which projects are likely to outperform the vast majority of others. A buyer can then layer in estimates of acquisition costs in order to ascertain disjunctions between price and quality. Price-to-quality rankings can help identify areas that may have been overlooked by competitors.

Participating in the best projects is no guarantee that a project will be profitable. A systemic crisis, such as low commodity prices, could adversely affect the entire focus area and render every project uneconomic. Even in this case, though, the best projects are likely to lose less money and be better positioned to bounce back when the crisis is resolved.

Other factors beyond technical or economic merit may also play a role in the top-down analysis. A project that is technically very highly rated in the comparative analysis may be subject to specific external risks that make it less attractive. A project may be located in a particularly unstable country. It could be subject to an international border dispute that prevents any company from being able to establish good title. Once a list of target projects is identified, projects that are precluded by such variables will need to be culled from the list.

It is precisely the possible presence of such variables that requires companies to undertake bottom-up due diligence as a secondary test. The bottom-up analysis generally ignores how the project compares to others in the focus area. Instead, the company seeks to evaluate all of the risks and variables that might come to bear on the possible project, assigns probabilities to each of them, and constructs economic models of alternatives. The principal categories of bottom-up analysis are technical, legal, and economic. Any of these might be risked in a manner that assigns probabilities to different outcomes.

TECHNICAL DUE DILIGENCE

Technical judgments about a project are at the heart of the top-down analysis, but those judgments are generally relativistic. In the bottom-up evaluation, technical judgments are more quantitative. Geologists, engineers, and other scientists must try to forecast the performance of a particular asset. This data is entered into a detailed economic model for a specific project.

In the petroleum sector, technical due diligence often entails projections of the recoverable reserves from a particular petroleum reservoir. Such estimates are based on seismic studies of the area and the results of wells that have been drilled. Reservoir engineers calculate how much oil can be recovered from the reservoir over its lifetime and establish production decline curves to forecast the amount of petroleum that will be produced in successive years. This production curve is one of the most important inputs to the bottom-up economic model.

The same basic approach is used to estimate throughput for pipelines in the midstream sector or for electricity in the downstream sector. Scientists may analyze the production potential of several different reservoirs as well as the capacities of competitive pipelines to ascertain how much petroleum will likely be available for a new pipeline or for a pipeline that is under consideration for acquisition. The economics of electricity plants may similarly be dependent on the demand for electricity from a particular market. Meteorologists may study weather patterns, demographers may consider population growth, and economists may calculate the economic demand for power—all with the goal of trying to ascertain how much power is likely to be sold in a market at different times of the year over a period of several years or decades.

In all of these cases, the judgment of technical personnel becomes paramount to success. Overestimations or underestimations in these fundamental factors have the potential to render your company's economic models inaccurate. As such, it is important for a company to undertake a careful process of checks and balances to ensure that the technical assumptions being included in its economic model are accurate. In the Gaille Method, I recommend that companies use two means of testing their technical assumptions: the risk-assessment method and the independent-voting method.

- *Risk-assessment method.* The risk-assessment method is an approach whereby the technical assumptions that are to be entered into any model are evaluated in a group setting. The presenters in this setting are the group of technicians working on the project and the audience is usually a selection of the company's most senior technical people who have no prior experience with the project being presented. The audience essentially acts as a review board for the project team's assumptions. Over the course of the risk-assessment meeting, the initial project assumptions are revised and new data emerges that reflect the consensus of both the project team and the senior scientists.

- *Independent-voting method.* The independent-voting method is a way for the business development group to further check assumptions. The independent-voting method begins before the project team has arrived at any consensus. At this early stage, it is likely that each member of the project team has arrived at an *individual* view that has not yet been tainted by the views of the broader group. During this window of time, it is possible for the company to poll the scientists and aggregate their individual views. This can be done through a formal process that secretly records each scientist's view on a ballot. It also can be done informally. For example, a business development executive can walk from office to office and record each team member's view. The company can then aggregate these views by averaging them. The average of independent views can be compared to the consensus views of the project team or the adjusted consensus view that reflects the overlay of the risk-assessment team. When there are substantial differences between the aggregated independent votes and the risk-assessment team, further investigation is warranted.

The scope of technical due diligence will depend on the nature of the project. An exploration project's technical due diligence will largely depend on a geological and geophysical examination of circumstantial and seismic data to determine the chance of finding petroleum on the prospect and, if petroleum is found, how much is there. As projects advance in their life cycles, the requirements of due diligence on the technical side expand. If the number of data points in the form of wells and project facilities increases, the amount of time it takes to complete due diligence—and its cost—increase accordingly.

A subset of the technical team will need to undertake environmental due diligence. In the exploration context, this might amount to environmental assessments such as the impact of seismic shooting on marine mammals or plans for controlling and managing a blowout. As a project advances, though, the prospect of aging facilities and historical degradation becomes a greater risk. Environmental due diligence in active projects might include examining baseline studies, required versus existing environmental permits and licenses, water and waste disposal practices, integrity of production facilities, history of incidents, air emissions, hazardous materials management (explosives, nuclear tools, etc.), and risk management and loss control programs.

Legal Due Diligence

The amount of legal due diligence required for a project depends on what is being acquired. If only an asset is being acquired, the focus of the due diligence is on the contracts granting rights to the asset. If there is a stock acquisition of one or more companies that own the asset, the legal due diligence requirements grow because those companies will have to be examined in detail to ensure that they hold no hidden liabilities or problems. Below is a high-level checklist of legal due diligence items that a business developer will usually need to consider:

- *Agreements related to the granting of rights.* In the petroleum context, these agreements would typically include all contracts between the seller and the government that concern the asset being acquired, such as concessions and production sharing contracts. With respect to midstream pipelines, these would include concessions, pipeline development agreements, and right-of-way agreements. Government agreements concerning power projects might include concession rights such as build-own-operate-transfer agreements, fuel supply agreements, and power purchase agreements.
- *Government approvals.* Often, government agreements are subject to further approvals such as decrees by the head of state, the council of ministers, or the nation's legislature. Legal due diligence includes determining from local counsel what approvals are required under the law and then checking the approval documents to ensure that they were properly obtained.
- *Foreign Corrupt Practices Act compliance.* During the due diligence process, a buyer will want to examine the history of the seller's relationship with the government to look for red flags that might indicate unlawful payments to government officials. The buyer will evaluate the seller's internal processes to protect against such payments and determine whether these processes have been followed with respect to the particular project. The buyer should also scrutinize any payments made to third-party consultants. Such consultants often serve as middlemen or fronts for illicit payments.
- *Joint venture agreements.* If the seller is not the only owner of the project, there likely will be many agreements and other documents in existence that relate to the joint operation

of the project, particularly the joint operating agreement. Further, some petroleum fields straddle multiple blocks, which can result in a second layer of agreements called "unitization agreements." This type of agreement is the commercial structure through which different groups of owners coordinate in the development of a single oil or gas field that stretches across two licensed areas.

- *Chain of title.* If the seller is not the original recipient of the grant of rights from the government, it will be important to review the chain of title for the asset, including prior sales and purchase agreements between the seller and the asset's previous owners.

- *Production sharing mechanism, royalty rights, fiscal terms, and tax liabilities and exemptions.* The government "take" mechanism must be researched and adequately understood so that the economic model accurately reflects when payments to the government must be made. The project might be exempted from certain taxes. These rights and obligations may be present in contracts, but they may also be buried in general provisions set forth in the country's laws. Local counsel will need to ensure that all of these obligations are identified and understood.

- *Encumbrances.* The buyer will need to determine whether there are any encumbrances on the assets that could be held in separate agreements or hidden in joint operating agreements or prior sale and purchase agreements. These include Area of Mutual Interest Agreements. Another concern is the presence of indirect nonworking interests such as net profits interests or royalties. These contractual obligations may not be reflected in the government agreements but may obligate a working interest owner to make substantial payments to companies that, for example, helped to secure the initial concession rights and are now no longer involved in the project. If any such obligations exist, they must be accurately reflected in the project economic model.

- *Commitments and minimum work obligations.* What are the legal obligations over time with respect to work programs and minimum expenditures? These will be important components of the economic model as they may impact the cost assumptions and the timing for expenditures.

- *Transferability.* Are there any restrictions on the contemplated transactions? The government's assignment approval process will need to be understood. The buyer will also want to know whether there are any preferential purchase rights applicable in favor of the government or other third parties.
- *Marketing rights.* Are there any restrictions on the sale or marketing of petroleum or pipeline capacity or electricity? Is the company required to sell all or a portion to the government? Are there price controls?
- *Guarantees.* The owner of an international petroleum project may need to provide specific guarantees of performance to the government, such as letters of credit or parent company guarantees.
- *Intellectual property.* Are there any licensed seismic and other technical data, software, and patents, copyrights, or trademarks?
- *Corporate due diligence.* With respect to any entities that may be acquired, an additional layer of due diligence is needed on each of those companies. Information to review for such entities includes: (1) name and jurisdiction; (2) articles of incorporation, bylaws, and similar documents (including any amendments, supplements, and attachments thereto); (3) all filings and correspondence with the government; (4) stock records and transfer books; (5) list of officers and directors; (6) minutes of board of directors and shareholder meetings; (7) agreements relating to options, voting trusts, warrants, subscriptions, and convertible securities; (8) list of countries in which the company is licensed or registered to do business, including a list of all branches and representative offices; (9) list of assets owned or leased (which, in most cases, should only relate to the petroleum asset being acquired); (10) if it is a subsidiary of a public company, list of all filings with the securities and exchange

commission of the home jurisdiction and the jurisdiction(s) in which it conducts business, as well as any annual reports that mention the subsidiary; and (11) list of outstanding powers of attorney and delegations of authority.

- *Debt arrangements.* Any loan or credit line arrangements should be reviewed and the project and company should be tested for compliance with the debt covenants set forth in the documents.

- *Labor agreements.* Will the buyer of the asset or company inherit any employment contracts? Are there any retirement plans or pensions? What are the severance rights and obligations? The laws of the host nation and the grant of rights from the government may require that a percentage of the workforce be local citizens. Is the seller in compliance?

- *Training, education, and social welfare obligations.* Are there any social welfare obligations, such as required support for training, education, or other programs?

- *Foreign exchange and currency controls.* To what extent does the host nation restrict foreign exchange and otherwise control currency movements? Can the company lift and sell its share of petroleum offshore and take possession of sales proceeds directly in offshore banks? To the extent that excess currency is deposited in the host nation's banking system, how easy is it to transfer funds out of the country?

- *Country legal review.* The legal department and outside counsel should review and consider applicable local laws and regulations.

- *Arbitration provisions.* The agreements should be reviewed for international arbitration provisions. In the event that some agreements are not governed by international arbitration, to what extent is the local judicial system functional?

- *Other regulations.* Is the project in regulatory compliance? Does the seller have the required licenses and permits? Has the seller been timely in making regulatory filings?

- *Other material contracts.* There may be other material arrangements unique to each project.
- *Other liabilities.* Any historical, existing, or threatened legal claims, disputes, and lawsuits will need to be examined.

BUSINESS AND FINANCIAL DUE DILIGENCE

There is a variety of commercial and financial issues that may fall outside the expertise of the company's technical and legal teams. These may include

- *Financial data.* The financial performance of the project and any related companies should be analyzed following a review of the applicable audited financial statements, production reports, operating costs, bank account statements, equipment and materials inventory, petroleum inventory, work programs and budgets, auditors' review letters, and annual management letters.
- *Labor and human resources.* The management organizational chart should be understood. The seller should provide a complete list of employees, designating which personnel are being transferred to the buyer with the project or project company.
- *Tax.* The business developer should obtain copies of the seller's tax returns and correspondence, waivers, or extensions, and a list of any ongoing or recent audits. Are there any tax liens?
- *Insurance.* The insurance coverage should be reviewed, including a list of existing coverage, expiry dates, and any recent claims activity.
- *Security risks.* The buyer should meet with the U.S. Embassy and other consultants to evaluate the security situation in the host nation and particular concerns in the vicinity of the project. Security issues may impact the project directly

(armed conflict) or indirectly (crime impacting employees after working hours).

- *Credit risks.* How creditworthy are the project's counterparties, including the government? In the event that a government expropriates the project, what overseas assets of the nation could be used to satisfy a judgment?
- *Political risks.* The host government's political risk should be considered. How stable has the government of the host nation been over time? To what extent does the population support the government and view it positively? Are there nationalistic tendencies? Is there hostility against foreign investment? Has the government historically respected the contractual and property rights of foreign investors? If there is a regime change, how likely is it that a new regime will respect the former regime's contractual arrangements?

The business developer may need to seek the support of other departments within the company, such as accounting, treasury, insurance, and security, to review these issues. If risks are identified, the company may retain outside consultants to provide a more detailed analysis.

ECONOMIC MODELS

The output of the due diligence process should be sufficient to construct an economic model. The economic model assimilates all of the technical, legal, and financial information about the asset and then forecasts cash flows and returns for the company. The following Figure 3.1 is a simplified economic model for a $50-million exploration program that culminates with the company achieving a 5 percent participating interest in a 500-million-barrel oil field.

Figure 3.1: Economic Model Output

YEAR	Gross Production MBOPD	Net Production MBOPD	Net Explor. Costs & PEP Overhead $M	Net Appraisal, Develop. Operations $M	Net Revenues $M	Net Cash Flow $M	Net After Tax Cash Flow $M
1	-	-	10000	0	-	(10,000)	(10,000.00)
2	-	-	10000	0	-	(10,000)	(10,000.00)
3	-	-	10000	17482	-	(27,482)	(27,482.08)
4	-	-	10000	42550	-	(52,550)	(52,550.00)
5	13	1	10400	10400	16,740	(3,660)	(3,659.89)
6	191	8	14365	14365	202,795	188,430	134,348.57
7	191	8	14365	14365	193,655	179,290	115,039.97
8	191	8	14365	14365	193,655	179,290	88,915.45
9	191	8	8876	8876	194,185	185,309	96,322.28
10	153	6	7103	7103	154,924	147,821	77,213.03
11	122	5	5703	5703	123,939	118,236	62,133.04
12	98	4	4584	4584	99,151	94,567	50,069.93
13	78	3	3698	3698	79,538	75,840	40,526.17
14	63	2	2972	2972	63,457	60,485	32,701.85
15	50	2	2398	2398	50,765	48,367	26,528.23
16	40	2	1834	1834	40,612	38,778	21,709.80
17	32	1	1471	1471	32,579	31,107	17,799.11
18	26	1	1174	1174	25,992	24,818	14,592.56
19	21	1	939	939	20,794	19,854	10,649.78
20	16	1	751	751	16,635	15,883	8,456.28
21	13	1	603	603	13,344	12,742	6,713.80
22	11	0	481	481	10,646	10,165	5,259.73
23	8	0	385	385	8,517	8,132	4,163.06
24	7	0	4752	4752	6,814	2,061	1,055.27
Reserves:	554 mmbo recov.	22 mmbo rec.	Net Totals:	161,251	1,548,736	1,337,486	710,506
			Gross Totals:	3,225,015	30,974,727	26,749,713	14,210,119

- *Gross production.* The gross production of the field is shown as the average number of barrels per day (in thousands of barrels) that the project is expected to produce in each year of its life based on the forecasts of the buyer's technical team. At the bottom of the table, the sum of the gross production reflects the recoverable reserves from the oil field (in millions of barrels). It is important that the recoverable reserves of a field not be confused with the original oil in place (OOIP), which is a considerably larger number than the recoverable reserves. Over time, different development projects will gradually recover more oil from the reservoir and the historical number of barrels recovered will often be reflected as a recovery percentage of the OOIP.
- *Net production.* This economic model operates on an oil field that is part of a tax royalty regime. Different fiscal regimes will be discussed in more detail later, but the primary point here is that before the prospective buyer can receive barrels from gross production, the government, under its petroleum

law, will deduct a percentage of those barrels as a royalty payment. The net production column reflects the company's 5 percent of production after this deduction.

- *Net exploration costs.* This column reflects the buyer's out-of-pocket costs for conducting its $50-million exploration program, including its 5 percent share of drilling costs on the well that it assumes will eventually expose the 500-million-barrel oil field.

- *Net appraisal, development, and operations costs.* These costs are 5 percent of the costs of developing and operating the discovery and its resulting field. These numbers may represent a combination of estimates by the buyer's and seller's technical teams.

- *Net revenues.* This represents the net production multiplied by an assumed oil price. The assumptions used in modeling commodity prices are closely guarded and vary from company to company. Some companies use flat commodity price assumptions, sometimes at conservative levels considerably below where future contracts may be trading. Other companies may develop elaborate commodity price curves that reflect various assumptions developed internally or externally (by consultants).

- *Net cash flow.* Net cash flow shows the difference between net revenues and all net costs incurred by the company in that year.

- *Net after-tax cash flow.* This number is the difference between net cash flow and the various taxes identified by legal due diligence as being applicable to the project's income stream.

Once a model has been achieved that generates a forecast of after-tax cash flow, the company can calculate the project's expected rate of return and net present value (NPV), which is the sum of the present values of the cash flow. Companies typically have a rate of return threshold for projects, below which the company will decline the project because it is not sufficiently profitable. The return threshold is also usually the discount rate used to ascertain the net present value. This enables the company to quickly determine whether a project meets its rate of return hurdle (a positive NPV equals yes) and how much profit beyond the return threshold will be produced (the value of the NPV calculation).

For example, if the company's rate of return hurdle were 10 percent, then it would likely use this same 10 percent as its discount rate in the NPV calculation. The NPV-10 analysis of the economic model would determine the present value of cash flows from the project in excess of this discount rate. In the simple economic model in our example, the NPV-10 calculation is approximately $250 million. By comparing the rates of return and the NPV-10s of various other projects, a company can more easily ascertain the relative wealth-producing effects of projects under consideration.

Economic models reflect assumptions, and assumptions usually carry with them probabilities of certain occurrences. As such, a critical element of project modeling is showing how the economic model, particularly the return and the NPV, may be affected by changes in the underlying assumptions. For example, how would higher or lower commodity prices change the project's economics? Typically, the economic model will provide alternative results for different price inputs, holding everything else constant. This comparison can indicate how sensitive the project is to falling commodity prices and how much upside the project holds if commodity prices rise.

That being said, this can be an academic exercise that is out of touch with the real world because of the interdependence of variables in a model. Changing one variable (such as price) in an economic model and holding other variables (such as costs) constant may be unrealistic. In the commodity price example, changes in product price can result in other assumptions in the model changing as well. Rising commodity prices correlate with development and operations cost inflation and with governments seeking to renegotiate commercial terms such as royalties and taxes. In other words, higher oil prices might not produce the return and NPV bonanza that one might expect.

Economists also may discount the results of an economic model through a risking process. This occurs in petroleum exploration economics, for example. Suppose a petroleum development has a net present value of $100 million if it is successful. However, success is contingent on the results of an exploration well proving that the possible reservoir identified by seismic data contains petroleum. Assume there is a 50 percent chance that the well will be successful (and the project will achieve a $100-million NPV) and a 50 percent chance that it will be a dry hole. If the well is dry, the project is worth nothing and is abandoned. Risked economics in this simple case would multiply the $100-million NPV by the chance that the project will be successful. This $50-million risked NPV also reflects the expected economic value of the project.

When a company is comparing various exploration opportunities, this metric can be useful for equalizing the playing field between exploration prospects that have differing characteristics of value and chance of success. For example, imagine a scenario where Block A has NPV of $500 million and a 15 percent chance of success ($75 million expected value) and Block B has NPV of $90 million with an 90 percent chance of success ($81 million expected value). The analysis would reveal that even though the projects have quite different risk and reward profiles, the expected economic value from both is about the same.

One problem with risked economic value comparisons is that the project with the best expected economic value might be inconsistent with a company's broader risk or reward goals. On the risk side of the equation, the expected economic value for a potential acquisition could be very high for a billion-barrel prospect with a low chance of success. Even if the expected economic value for such a project is the highest in a group under consideration, it might not fit the company's risk tolerance profile.

Similar disjunctions can occur with respect to the size of the rewards a company is seeking. In the expected economic value analysis, small projects can appear to have about the same or even better NPV than much larger projects due to the effect of discounting on the larger projects. Materiality is an important consideration for large companies. Such companies need to evaluate whether the acquisition would economically matter and to take care that the expected economic value calculations are not distracting from materiality considerations.

CONCLUSION

Project evaluations are best undertaken using both top-down and bottom-up evaluations. The top-down process is designed to cull the focus area universe down to a more manageable short list of projects. When projects on the target list become available, a bottom-up due diligence process should be undertaken. The bottom-up process varies depending on the nature of the project but typically includes technical, legal, financial, and economic components. The top-down process should provide your company with the comfort that, of all the projects like this one in the world, the project in question is among the best. Bottom-up due diligence should confirm that the initial analysis is correct and that there are no aspects of the project that might compromise its value.

CHAPTER 4

THE HOST GOVERNMENT RELATIONSHIP

E very interaction between a company and a government is important. A bad first impression can result in the government not allowing a company to purchase an asset. Even after a company has acquired energy resources, problems with the government relationship can lead to loss of concession rights or, at a minimum, being blocked from participation in future energy projects. Corruption must be avoided, too. In light of such risks, a business development executive should proactively manage all aspects of the government relationship to ensure that the company maintains good standing in each nation where it owns or seeks energy projects.

THE PROBLEM OF THE OUTSIDER

Technological advances such as the Internet, mobile phones, and satellite television are homogenizing disparate communities around the world. Suits and ties in business meetings are gradually becoming commonplace in regions where traditional clothing was once the norm. Most oil ministers around the world are highly educated, fluent in English, watch cable news channels, and are immersed in the American entertainment culture of music, television, and movies. Beneath the surface, however, subtle cultural differences abound and it is important not to offend a government host.

The use of the word *host* cannot be emphasized enough. When an organization enters a country other than its own and engages in business there, it is a guest. Its privilege of doing business there can be easily lost if it fails to act professionally and in accordance with the host country's conventions. In 2010, British Petroleum (BP) learned this lesson in the United States following the Deepwater Horizon oil spill. Tony Hayward, BP's chief executive officer, demonstrated typical British reserve and sought to downplay the spill. Americans viewed many of his remarks as insensitive.

If one of the largest oil companies in the world can stumble on the stage of international relations with a country that shares the same language and a similar cultural history, imagine the potential pitfalls that can arise on more distant shores. For example, colors can have vastly different meanings around the world. In China, red is a symbol of celebration and good luck, whereas in parts of Africa it is the color of mourning. On one occasion, while en route to an African nation, I read a report on the local culture that noted that the color red was viewed negatively. I had packed two ties for my meetings with the oil minister: one red and one pink. To be on the safe side, I visited the duty-free shop in Paris and bought ties in yellow and green. To avoid the possibility of offense, it is important to research the cultural and political history of a nation. There are many regional, and even country-specific, books that provide guidance on doing business in different parts of the world.

The Initial Meeting

International governments can be particularly sensitive to the formality of contact. Americans reflexively initiate contact with telephone calls or e-mails and then tend to follow up with more formal communications and face-to-face meetings. This approach can be viewed as cavalier or even disrespectful by foreign governments. As a general rule, you should approach the first meeting with a foreign government as follows:

- About two months in advance of a trip, you work with the U.S. Embassy in the country to identify the appropriate ministers to meet with.
- You send letters of introduction by courier to each official explaining that you would like to visit them and will soon be requesting a meeting through the U.S. Embassy.
- Through its Gold Key Service, the U.S. Embassy contacts schedulers for the officials and produces an agenda. A typical schedule will include meetings with: (1) the U.S. ambassador and economic officers at the Embassy, who will provide a briefing on political affairs, security issues, and the status of the country's relationship with the United States, including any outstanding issues or disputes between the governments; (2) the oil minister, executives from the state oil company, and other important government officials in the energy sector; (3) government officials representing the finance sector, including the finance minister and officials responsible for increasing foreign investment; (4) government officials representing the executive officer, who may be the head of state or prime minister but more likely is one or the other's chief of staff; and (5) other U.S. companies and expatriates in the country who can discuss their experiences and problems doing business and living there.
- Upon arrival, a Gold Key Service representative usually meets you at the airport to provide the escort of a commercial services staff member. If the official language of the nation is not English, the escort acts as an interpreter; otherwise, Gold Key Services can assist in locating one. Even if the official speaks English, it is an important sign of respect for a visitor to be accompanied by an interpreter. It gives the official the

option to speak in his or her own language and ensures that communications will flow smoothly if other non-English speakers join the meeting.

- The Gold Key Service escort helps guide you on protocol and ensures that you do not run afoul of any cultural issues during the meetings. Each meeting with a government official should begin with a description of your company, some information about your background and role in the company, and an explanation of why your organization is interested in doing business in the host country. If possible, the particular projects of interest should be identified. In the case of energy sector officials, this will usually commence a dialogue about these projects or perhaps about others that the official believes might interest your company. At the end of the meeting, you should leave some materials about your organization, translated into the official language of the host government, if possible.

- Demeanor in meetings with senior government officials is important, too. Present yourself and your company with authority—without being disrespectful. As a consequence of the legacy of colonialism and the arrogance of Americans or Europeans who have preceded you, it is not uncommon for officials to be wary and even defensive about the slightest indication that you or your company knows how to develop their resources better than they do. As such, you should emphasize words such as collaboration, partnership, and teamwork and always keep in mind that a nation's natural resources are its own.

- Either before or after meetings, you should spend some time visiting cultural and natural sights in the country, including some that are outside of the capital city. This conveys respect and interest for the host nation's resources. It also enables you to obtain a better feel for what the country is like away from the government and business sectors. Traveling around the country provides a feeling for the quality of road and air infrastructure.

- Upon your return to the United States, you should send thank-you letters to each person you met with. In the case of government officials, thank-you notes should be translated. You reiterate in these letters any areas or projects that are of interest to your company.

Author Pictured in the North West Frontier Province of Pakistan

At the initial meeting, the groundwork is laid for a future acquisition. The government is able to put a face with the name of your company. You have an opportunity to capture the attention of your host and talk about your company's experience and expertise. You can even explain what types of projects your company would like to acquire in the host country.

COUNTRY ENTRY

Once your company has acquired an interest in a project, the next set of meetings will be considerably easier. You have already told the host government of your company's plans to acquire an asset, and when you return to seek their approval, the process will be more straightforward because of the existing relationship. You will immediately be viewed as reasonably credible because you informed the host of your plans and carried them through. In other words, you are a company that does what it says.

The second set of meetings generally includes representatives from your company and from the seller's. Prior to this meeting, it is important that the transaction between your organizations be kept out of the media or otherwise leaked to the government. If the host government hears about a transaction involving its energy assets from a source other than the buyers and sellers involved, it can be construed as offensive. Imagine if the president of a country learns from the Internet that company X is divesting its assets in the host country to company Y. The president will be surprised and offended to discover that he appears to be the last to hear about dispositions of his own nation's resources. He will complain to the oil minister and the oil minister in turn will express dissatisfaction with both companies.

The underlying sensitivity relates to the fact that natural resources generally belong to a nation and its people and are often are viewed as a national treasure. Most petroleum codes and petroleum agreements require that the government approve any transfer of resource rights from one company to another. Whenever a company announces that it has undertaken a transaction before the government has been informed, the implication is that the government does not matter or, worse, that you may be trying to do a deal behind the government's back. The reflex of the government is then to exercise its power, which can result in a slower approval process or even a denial.

At your second meeting with the government, explain that the buying and selling companies would like to complete the transaction—assuming that the government supports and approves of it. Both companies should be careful to repeatedly state that they are seeking the government's approval. The goals of the meeting should be to solicit the official's support in the approval process, to obtain the official's views on how the approval process will work, and to ascertain what additional information the government may need in order to undertake its evaluation of the proposed transaction.

Differences may exist between the formal approval process set forth in the petroleum code/agreements and the practical one followed by the government. This is one reason it is important to preview all actions with the appropriate officials before filing any formal documents. Some nations may have informal advisors or review processes that are not part of statutory or regulatory law. These advisors may need to be included in the process and your company may be required to meet with them before they make a recommendation to the minister or president.

The resource assignment approval process causes the most grief for international energy companies. No matter what the laws, regulations, or contracts say, the government has the discretion to allow a transaction to go forward or to block it. If the government does not want your company involved in the project or wants another company instead, there may be nothing you can do.

Even if the host government likes your company, the seller may have had historical problems with the government that you know nothing about. Sometimes these problems rise to such a level that it expedites the approval process because the government wants the selling company to leave the country. Other times, the government may not cooperate with a transaction because of a poor (historical) relationship. For example, there were industry rumors that a supermajor's multibillion-dollar offer to buy a smaller company's interest in a major African field was derailed in part by the acrimonious personal history between some of the seller's executives and the oil minister.

The time it might take for a host government to approve or deny projects can be frustratingly slow. I had an acquisition in West Africa with a supermajor, and it took almost one year to obtain approval. There were no particular issues with the proposal other than the government had higher priorities than our transaction. We conceived an indirect strategy whereby one of my responsibilities was to track the oil minister's international speaking engagements. Over the course of that year, I heard the minister speak on three continents. Each time I sat in the front row, and whenever his speech was over, I walked up, said hello, and inquired about our project.

Beyond the approval of the transfer, there will likely be many smaller government and regulatory actions required before your company is fully licensed to do business in the host nation. A buyer will need the assistance of local counsel to navigate each nation's labyrinth of requirements for foreign participation. This might include forming and capitalizing a local corporation. A local company or an offshore company may be required to obtain various permits such as business, tax, employment, and environmental licenses. There usually is not much discretion involved in the granting of these types of secondary permits. It is just a matter of ensuring that the filings are made and that someone follows up on a weekly basis to ensure that they progress as quickly as possible through the bureaucracy.

ONGOING GOVERNMENT COMPLIANCE ISSUES

Once a transaction is approved, the relationship with the government is ongoing and must be carefully managed. This includes compliance with the project contracts and the laws and regulations of the host nation. Issues around compliance may include

- Obtaining government approval of work programs and budgets for a project
- Obtaining government approval of development plans
- Obtaining government approval of well locations or pipeline routes
- Obtaining government approval of production or throughput schedules
- Compliance with local supply obligations, which may require the sourcing and purchasing of equipment and materials from locally owned companies
- Compliance with local hiring preferences (and exceeding those standards, if possible), which may require the hiring and staffing of operations with local citizens
- Compliance with import regulations with respect to equipment and supplies

- Compliance with banking regulations on currency conversion and export
- Compliance with visa and residency rules for expatriate residents

It is also important to ensure that employees and contractors comply with the laws in their personal lives. Laws pertaining to alcohol and sexual conduct may be dramatically different in other nations. In the Middle East, certain regions may appear permissive on the surface, but may from time to time make examples of those who violate their laws. Expatriates have occasionally been arrested and charged with crimes for public displays of affection such as kissing. Similarly, some countries ban driving with any amount of alcohol in the bloodstream or even the possession of alcohol at all.

One of the more unusual cases of running afoul of local law occurred in Libya. Shortly after American sanctions were lifted, a hotel in Tripoli was launching a new fine dining restaurant. As part of its marketing campaign, the hotel ordered several large billboards showing a photo of the hotel's Filipino chef holding a silver platter of food. Unfortunately, Libyan law made it a serious crime to depict any person other than Colonel Gaddafi on billboards. The origin of the law stemmed from efforts to prevent political dissent and from the desire of the ruling party to convey its power through images of Colonel Gaddafi. The hotel's local counsel alerted the executive team to this law and the billboard campaign was abandoned. Had it gone through, the populace of Tripoli would have awakened to a smiling man wearing white and offering platters of food. Was this their new leader? The general counsel of the hotel quipped, "Coup de chef."

THE IMPORTANCE OF GOOD COMMUNICATION

The stability of a company's relationship with the host government requires open communication channels. Unfortunately, officials may be hesitant to directly raise issues or problems. This reluctance to confront may stem from wanting to avoid conflict, fear of offending the guest company, the belief that the problem was a one-time occurrence and will go away on its own, or fear that the matter will reflect poorly on the official whose responsibility it is to regulate.

Reluctance to quickly and directly confront a problem can create a cascade of issues. It may become more difficult, or impossible, to address the government's concern if it waits months or years to raise it. Such deferrals also set the stage for a company to make the same mistake again and again, thereby repeatedly offending the government because no one has told the company that there is a problem. One day a dispute or major issue will arise, and the organization will suddenly hear about dozens of errors and omissions committed over many years. Although every mistake a company makes might be documented by officials, the company is not always informed.

In my experience, the best way to avoid these types of surprises is to cultivate excellent one-on-one relationships with individual officials. This extends not only to the relationship with the executive or minister, but throughout the company's hierarchy, all the way down to project engineers and geologists. The relaxed environment of social engagements such as tennis, golf, and dinner can open a flow of communication that may be stymied in the conference room. Moreover, these are the moments when the company's personnel should ask, "Is there anything you think we could be doing better?" It enables the official to indirectly and informally alert a company to the presence of an issue.

CORRUPTION

Corruption occurs when a government official is induced by a company to make a decision that is in the official's best interest rather than the government's best interest. Consider the case where an oil minister is responsible for awarding a concession to explore for oil and there are a dozen companies competing. There may be qualitative and quantitative elements to the various companies' proposals. Certain companies may be offering the government larger signing bonuses or may have more capital or better track records of discovering petroleum than others. In an ideal world, the minister will weigh these factors from the perspective of the *nation* and select the company that he or she believes provides the best package for the *nation*. What happens if Company A offers the oil minister a $1-million bribe (payable to him personally)? The oil minister's decision-making process is then distorted as he is induced to think about his own well-being rather than that of the nation. If Company A obtains the license through a bribe, the nation may be worse off because its bonus payment may be smaller than that offered by another company or the quality of the exploration may be lower.

Over the past three decades, the world has grown less tolerant of corruption. In 1977, the United States enacted the Foreign Corrupt Practices Act (FCPA), which makes it a crime to offer anything of value to a foreign official for the purposes of inducing such person to not perform his or her duty or to otherwise obtain advantage. This statute has been repeatedly enforced against both companies and individuals, with many convictions obtained. Individuals working in the international energy arena need to be aware of the FCPA and similar statutes in other jurisdictions. There is no deal that is worth violating the FCPA and going to prison.

Practically speaking, laws such as the FCPA have made corruption less visible. Whereas older hands in the industry recount tales of high-ranking officials asking for personal payments in conjunction with deals, this is less common now. Ministers and deputy ministers are more likely to be aware of the restrictions on American and European companies. They know that asking for a bribe will result in a negative answer and quite possibly lead to complaints being made to their superiors. In other words, the likelihood of such an overture being successful is low—and it entails considerable risk.

Requests for payments are much more likely to come from low-level bureaucrats in the context of operating an energy project where minor approvals are needed or goods are being imported into the country. These types of requests often involve a government official who refuses to do his duty until he is paid. For example, an official in the immigration department may refuse to approve a visa until he is personally paid. The FCPA has a special exception for this type of facilitating payment. When the action is ordinary and does not require any special consideration, payment to receive the action is not considered a bribe. This is consistent with the idea that corruption is essentially akin to paying an official to *not* do his or her job. A facilitating payment is made to get someone to do his or her job.

The most difficult cases involve middlemen or fronting companies in which government officials may have an economic interest. These kinds of arrangements can be hard to detect because it may appear to be a legitimate transaction with a private citizen. Local consultants from the host nation often use their relationships with key government officials to advance the agenda of foreign companies. These local representatives may be highly compensated with cash or equity, just as a lobbyist might be in the United States. How can an American company be certain that its local representatives are not using part of the lobbying payments to bribe foreign officials to garner favor for their clients? At the outset, it is important that all such representatives be under a service agreement that prohibits them from passing along any payments to government officials. It also is important for these individuals to be educated about the FCPA and bribery and that due diligence is undertaken to ensure that they have good reputations.

CONCLUSION

Any company doing business in another region must keep in mind that it is a guest and the nation is its host. The company must be on its best behavior and should be sensitive to cultural differences that could highlight its outsider status. Ideally, each company considering doing business in a foreign country should arrange an introductory visit before any assets are acquired, which will smooth the government approval process later. Following an acquisition, the buyer of an asset should arrange a second visit to inform the government of the contemplated transaction and respectfully seek its approval. Once the project is underway, the government's focus shifts to that of regulator and it is essential that the company comply with its obligations and maintain open channels of communication with officials. Corruption is a much greater risk in the international environment, and the organization must be careful to take precautions to ensure that improper direct or indirect payments are not made to government officials.

CHAPTER 5

THE NATURAL RESOURCE CURSE

conomists have observed that countries rich in natural resources have often experienced less economic growth than countries lacking in them. There does not appear to be a single cause of this phenomenon and some countries with abundant natural resources have done better than others. The reasons why the resource curse affects one country more than another are not well understood. Corruption, self-dealing by political leaders, and weak institutions appear to matter. Governments flush with resource revenue may not invest in policies that are likely to foster long-term growth. Meanwhile, the labor and capital demands of the energy industry may be slowly drawing resources from other sectors, thereby weakening those legs of the economy. These and other factors seem to suppress economic growth to varying degrees, particularly in developing nations. When a company enters a new country, it is important to examine the overall economy and try to understand how the host nation has sought to address these risks in the past and how it has been affected (or not) by the resource curse.

WHY THE RESOURCE CURSE MATTERS

When a company enters a new territory, it is useful to understand how its economy is faring. Is the country experiencing economic contraction or growth? At what pace? Which sectors are contracting or growing? Relatively speaking, which sectors account for what percentage of the economy? How large is the energy sector in relation to the others? When energy is coupled with other natural resources, what percentage of the economy is natural resource–based?

If natural resources are a significant or dominant component of the country's economy, the next line of inquiry is to understand how the host government manages the revenues from natural resource extraction. Unlike other sectors, the extraction of natural resources is subject to a depletion curve. However abundant those resources are when they are discovered, each day of production spends those resources and one day they will be gone. Essentially, the natural resource wealth of a nation is converted into liquid currency slowly over time.

In such cases, a nation will have a track record regarding how it has managed its liquidity. Has the nation reinvested the liquidity with an eye toward providing for long-term growth? Or have politicians embezzled or squandered large amounts of the extractive revenues? The extent to which revenues have been managed wisely or poorly will likely impact a company's international operations in a variety of ways.

The presence of the resource curse can undermine the stability of a government and the nation itself. The greater the discontent of the population with the economy or the management of resources by the government, the higher is the probability that there will be regime change or even civil war. If the government that granted a company rights to a project ceases to exist, the new government may or may not recognize those rights and the project could be subject to expropriation or substantial erosion of its economic value. As such, companies should be cognizant that the resource curse is a real and significant risk to realizing the return of their investment.

Niger Delta Oil Fields[1]

The resource curse can make it challenging to operate and otherwise do business in a region. The absence of investment in infrastructure and transportation can make it difficult to travel (or safely travel). Low investment in education can require a company to hire and house costly expatriate labor. Lack of manufacturing can result in expensive importation of goods and equipment. Poverty, underinvestment in law enforcement, and discontent can increase criminal activity and violence against energy companies. These types of risks need to be considered at the time of the investment decision.

---

1 *Nigeria Militants Blow Up Two Oil, Gas Pipelines,* www.dalje.com (May 17, 2009), http://dalje.com/en-world/nigeria-militants-blow-up-two-oil-gas-pipelines/258630.

APPROACHES TO MANAGING THE RESOURCE CURSE

It is also important to examine what efforts, if any, a nation has taken to mitigate the resource curse over time. Has the host government ignored the issue entirely, or has it enacted measures, successful or not, in an effort to manage the problem? Has it participated in any international initiatives or charters? However quixotic such measures may be, they are valuable indicators of the intentions of the government and may lessen the resentment that can manifest among the population in the wake of naked embezzlement of wealth by leaders.

The mechanisms that nations have used to address the resource curse include

- *Trusts.* This approach can be structured in many ways, but generally seeks to separate the management of resource revenues from the usual political process. For example, segregated accounts could be established within the nation or at a foreign bank. These arrangements typically include a board of directors that is responsible for investment decisions apart from the usual budgetary process. The trust may be subject to statutory guidelines regarding how much of the principal can be spent in a year and what activities it may be spent on (such as health care or education). To varying degrees, the trust mechanism is designed to insulate the nation's resource wealth from political expediency, weak institutions, and embezzlement.
- *Direct payments.* While a trust program essentially creates an additional layer of bureaucracy (which hopefully makes better decisions than the existing government institutions), direct payments seek to remove institutions from the equation entirely. Under a direct payment approach, resource revenues are paid directly to the people. Alaska has a form of direct payment. Its residents receive equal annual payments from the state's petroleum fund. Direct payments could also be made only to specific individuals whose property is affected by the extraction, in much the same way that private

landowners in the United States receive royalty payments from petroleum production on their property.

- *Transparency initiatives.* There are various initiatives that seek to increase the transparency and accountability of natural resource revenues through disclosures by companies, governments, and financial institutions. Transparency initiatives all share the general goal of decreasing corruption and mismanagement. These include the Publish What You Pay, Extractive Industries Transparency, and Publish What You Lend initiatives. The 2009 Natural Resource Charter advocates certain economic guidelines for how governments should best develop and make use of their natural resources.

How to Work with the Host Government to Better Manage the Resource Curse

Once a company has decided to invest in a nation suffering from the resource curse, it is faced with the question of whether to have a dialogue with the host government about the issue. The general approach of most companies is to leave the governing to officials and be a passive (or reactive) participant in the consequences of their decisions. This approach has the advantage of removing a potential point of friction in the relationship between a government and the company and avoids having political differences spill over into an otherwise successful commercial relationship. After all, any time a guest company gives its host nation advice on governing, it runs the risk of sounding paternalistic or colonial.

That being said, the extraction of resources by a company is one of the *causes* of the resource curse. Should the extractor company put blinders on and ignore how its activities affect the communities and people of the host nation? Particularly in the case of a country where your company is the initial developer of substantial resources, it would be reasonable to have a dialogue with senior government officials about the impact of the project on the nation's future.

A key component of this dialogue is a company's ability to offer a concrete proposal that is limited in scope to the energy project being undertaken. In my 2011 *Energy Law Journal* article "Mitigating the Resource Curse: A Proposal for a Microfinance and Educational Lending Royalty Law," I described an alternative approach that would divert a small percentage of energy project revenues to microfinance and educational lending programs.[2] I discussed how such lending programs have been successfully implemented in the developing world and how they specifically counteract the way extractive industries undermine investment in education and other economic sectors.

My article focused on the nationwide implementation of a royalty, but the microfinance royalty approach also could be implemented on a project-by-project basis. Many production-sharing contracts have social expenditure obligations whereby petroleum companies are required to make annual expenditures for the construction of local clinics or schools or to fund petroleum industry training programs for local residents so that they can eventually obtain employment in the project. The intent of these programs is to improve the quality of life in the communities impacted by onshore petroleum extraction. As petroleum development has moved offshore, the local impact tends to diminish in comparison to the resource curse. I negotiated a production-sharing contract for a deepwater African block where the community obligation was replaced with a general scholarship fund precisely because the nearest community was unlikely to even be aware of the existence of the development many miles over the horizon.

In such cases of deepwater extraction, or as a supplement to existing community programs, a production-sharing contract could include a microfinance and educational lending royalty as part of the package of economic terms and conditions. In my article, I proposed a modest 0.50 percent royalty for each of the two programs, which I argued had the twin virtues of being both an amount that is politically realistic and that generates enough revenue to make a difference in the areas of microfinance and educational

---

2 Scott Gaille, *Mitigating the Resource Curse: A Proposal for a Microfinance and Educational Lending Royalty Law*, 32 ENERGY LAW JOURNAL 81 (2011).

lending. In the context of a production-sharing agreement, similar considerations apply because it is likely that the cost of the royalty will be shared between the company and the government. The company will benefit from the small royalty because its practical result will be to marginally increase the economic development of the nation over the multidecade life of the petroleum development. The government will benefit because it will be able to promote the royalty as a direct benefit to the people.

Will such a royalty matter? If we consider a petroleum development that will average 50,000 barrels of oil per day at a sale price of $75 per barrel, this amounts to gross revenues of about $1.3 billion per year, of which 1 percent is about $13 million. Assuming this would be expended on college scholarships in the United States at a cost of $30,000 per year for four years, it would fund more than four hundred student scholarships annually. The introduction of similar amounts of capital into microfinance lending could build a substantial lending base for local entrepreneurs. Over the lifetime of a twenty-year project, the royalty would amount to a quarter of a billion dollars being injected into microfinance and/or educational lending programs.

CONCLUSION

The resource curse arises when the extractive sector of an economy distorts and stunts the development of other economic sectors. This is thought to result from a number of causes, including the availability of low-skilled but high-paying employment opportunities in the resource sector that can decrease the incentive of the host country (and individuals) to invest in human capital required by other economic sectors. When a company enters a new country, it is important to evaluate to what extent the economy has been adversely affected by the resource curse and what steps the nation has taken to diversify its economy and to use portions of its petroleum wealth to advance sectors. How are the government's petroleum revenues accounted for and to what extent are citizens participating in the wealth being created by energy development? If the government is willing to engage in a dialogue about the natural resource curse, it may be possible for one or more oil companies to take the lead and implement their own plan, such as a small 1 percent royalty divided among educational and entrepreneurial lending. By proposing such a plan, a company conveys to the government that it is seeking to be a long-term partner in the economy of the host nation.

CHAPTER 6

THE EMERGENCE OF NATIONAL OIL COMPANIES

Relationships with host governments are further complicated by the fact that many governments have established their own national oil companies. Unlike an oil ministry, which acts as a regulator, a national oil company (NOC) is a commercial enterprise that may compete with private energy companies both within and outside of the host nation. If the NOC has the capability to develop a project in its home nation, it may be shown favoritism in the awarding of the project. Even outside its own borders, the NOC may have advantages over private competitors. Nation-to-nation diplomacy may result in concessions being awarded to another country's NOC in the hope of winning favors such as loans or other forms of investment.

National oil companies usually do not play by the same economic rules as private companies. NOCs may be more concerned with accessing resources—or employing their own citizens—than with profitability. In a competitive bidding situation where an NOC's goal is resource security rather than profits for investors, it may pay a premium for that security that would generate negative economics for a private oil company. This results in NOCs being formidable competition on the international stage.

THE NOC WITHIN ITS BORDERS

National oil companies vary from publicly traded behemoths like Petrobras with market capitalizations in the billions of dollars to Seychelles Petroleum, which manages the resources and fuel for a nation of 85,000 people. What an NOC can do within its own nation's boundaries largely depends on its ability to access capital. The greater an NOC's ability to access capital, the more likely it is that the NOC has had the opportunity to acquire the personnel and technical expertise needed to operate.

NOCs typically start with funding from sovereign wealth, as another line in the government's budget. At the incubation stage, an NOC may not be much more than a handful of employees in a small office with low overhead costs and no independent source of revenues. As foreign oil companies come into the nation to explore for petroleum resources, the NOC is typically granted participating interests in the concessions awarded to the outside companies. These interests are perhaps 5, 10, or 20 percent of each concession and are initially "carried" (i.e., the NOC's costs are paid by the foreign contractor)—at least through the exploration phase. This gives the NOC the right to participate in joint operating committee meetings and the opportunity for its personnel to learn more about the nation's geology and exploration prospects. If the exploration well is a dry hole, the NOC learns at little or no cost to the government. When a discovery is made, however, the landscape may start to change as the NOC's revenue stream expands dramatically. The NOC gains reserves, production, and, most importantly, cash flow to take itself to levels that its nation could not spare from the general revenue funds. In this way, the host government is able to use the foreign oil company to effectively finance the next stage of growth for the NOC.

With independent revenues comes the capacity to hire more people and to perhaps finance its own exploration programs through the use of contracts with service companies. The reserves and revenues attributable to the state oil company may give it the financial capability to establish debt facilities without any requirement of government guarantee. The presence of this wealth may also enable the NOC to access the public markets and raise capital through initial public offerings (IPOs) and secondary stock offerings to international investors. NOCs such as Sinopec have market capitalizations in the billions and can access a range of capital channels to fund their growth—from sovereign wealth to schoolteachers in California. Such companies have reached a point where they can fund and operate multibillion-dollar projects without the need to partner with private companies such as Exxon, Total, or Shell.

As an NOC's capability grows, it first becomes a competitor for foreign oil companies within its own nation's borders. Why should a nation share its production with foreign oil companies if its own NOC has the capability to develop the same resource on a 100-percent ownership basis? What tends to happen is that more and more projects are steered toward the local company, beginning with simpler or smaller projects. Foreign oil companies' expiring concession rights on long-lived fields may be transferred to the NOC, further fueling its revenue growth. Eventually, the NOC is likely to be in a position where it has the pick of the lowest risk development and exploration, thereby pushing the foreign companies further to the sidelines, where marginal economics and high risk exploration are the only opportunities left.

THE NOC OUTSIDE OF ITS BORDERS

While it may be expected for a nation to favor its state-owned oil company and try to incubate its growth, such companies are increasingly becoming competitive outside their own borders.

NOCs may be financed with sovereign revenue backing to engage in extraterritorial acquisitions that are in the nation's interest. Such projects could advance national security through the acquisition of petroleum reserves or through providing additional employment opportunities for citizens. Even in the absence of sovereign financial backing, an NOC with sufficient success at home can leverage its technical experience and production revenue stream to compete for projects elsewhere. The very assets that are granted to the state oil company by its sovereign owner often enable it to access financing channels in the form of debt or securities offerings in the same way that private companies seek to fund their own acquisitions. Thus, the ability of a state oil company to access financial resources may be the same as, or even greater than, a comparable-sized private oil company.

The state-owned oil company might have other advantages, as well. Profits may be a consideration, but other noneconomic goals play an important role. For example, if a sovereign oil company is seeking to secure oil and gas reserves for the nation's economic security, the profitability of the project may be of secondary importance. Whereas a private oil company's investors would likely demand rate-of-return thresholds in the high teens, the NOC may view a break-even project as attractive because it can secure large reserves for its sovereign owner. This difference in economics can enable the NOC to pay a higher acquisition price for the same project (as compared with a private company).

An additional issue that arises is the political dynamics between two nations. When one nation is considering whether to award a petroleum project to a private oil company or another nation's state oil company, it must consider how its relationship with the sovereign owner might be improved. The sovereign owner might be able to offer benefits to the host nation beyond mere development of the energy project, such as loans or foreign aid.

While these may be advantages for NOCs, the host government has to balance higher up-front acquisition payments and possible political benefits against the relative technical capability of the alternative companies vying for a project. A host government wants to know that its natural resources will be developed efficiently. The fact that an NOC may pay an outsize bonus to be awarded an exploration block provides little solace if the NOC cannot discover, develop, and produce petroleum. The returns from successful exploration and development are in the many billions of dollars and far outstrip the up-front payment differential offered by NOCs at the bid round stage. The exploration successes of private oil and gas companies are formidable, and a host government may well opt for the private oil company's technical expertise and track record over the incremental rents offered by the NOC.

Moreover, there is a potential incentive among NOCs to acquire resource rights with the intention of developing them years into the future. This is consistent with the resource acquisition model of nations such as China. Whereas a private oil company has a clear incentive to generate returns as soon as possible for its investors, an NOC may sit on potential reserves for purposes of multidecade national security. From a host government's perspective, this can prove problematic in the developing world. Budgets may depend on timely development of natural resources, and the desire of developing nations to rapidly access the revenues from petroleum projects (whether for the enrichment of the ruling group or the advancement of the nation) may be more aligned with the goals of private oil companies than those of national oil companies. While national oil companies may have advantages in the initial capture of petroleum licenses, diverging incentives or capability over the longer term may counteract them. A more detailed discussion of these issues can be found in my 2010 *Energy Law Journal* article "Allocation of International Petroleum Licenses to National Oil Companies: Insights from the Coase Theorem."[3]

CONCLUSION

National oil companies raise two sets of issues—those relating to their role in the host country and issues faced abroad. Governments

---

3 Scott Gaille, *Allocation of International Petroleum Licenses to National Oil Companies: Insights from the Coase Theorem*, 31 ENERGY LAW JOURNAL 111 (2010).

view NOCs as having the potential to increase the percentage of their take in the development of domestic natural resources. Whereas a government without an NOC may have to give up perhaps 50 percent of the revenues from its natural resources to foreign companies, the creation of a viable state oil company enables it to participate more aggressively in development and to retain a greater share of the resource wealth locally. In other circumstances, NOCs can be used to advance a government's policies outside of its borders. An NOC with extensive projects overseas can be, for example, an employer of citizens or a vehicle for national security. In either case, a business development executive must be aware of the role that NOCs play and how their incentives may differ from those of other petroleum companies.

CHAPTER 7

THE ROLE OF
JOINT VENTURES

C entral to the petroleum industry is the practice of partnerships. Even the largest companies in the world routinely sell portions of their assets to other organizations for purposes of entering into joint ventures. The frequency with which petroleum projects are owned by multiple companies, often fierce competitors, can be difficult to explain to those more familiar with another industry. At its heart, the partnering approach is driven by the twin characteristics of high risk and large capital expenditure. This results in a high frequency of partnership arrangements as companies seek to diversify their risks and share in funding obligations. Partnering is typically executed through joint operating agreements, which provide a framework for the sharing of costs and revenues for a petroleum project. When there are multiple companies participating in a development, one must be designated the operator. This company leads and executes the petroleum project. The other organizations (nonoperators) may have various approval rights, but generally are along for the ride, paying their pro rata share of costs and receiving their pro rata share of petroleum revenues.

Partnership Drivers

Petroleum extraction begins with exploration, where there is a substantial risk that a well being drilled will be a dry hole. This is, for the most part, a binary game. Either a well provides a discovery (and is usually worth many multiples of the risked capital) or it is a dry hole and all of the investment is lost. To put this in perspective, a typical international exploration well has between a one-in-five and one-in-six chance of success. There is an 80 percent or greater chance that all of the investment will be lost. Moreover, the cost of a well is typically in the many millions of dollars, with costs reaching more than $100 million per well in deepwater exploration.

A petroleum company can make an investment of $100 million on a single well with an 80 percent chance of losing that investment or it can diversify that $100 million investment across five such wells with a 20 percent ownership interest in each well. The difference in probability of complete failure—that is, of the wells being dry holes—can be dramatically reduced through the creation of a portfolio. In the first case, the company has an 80 percent chance of losing its $100 million and in the second case, it has about a one-third chance of losing that amount.

What is left out of the above example is the value of the success case. A major deepwater discovery can have a net present value of $15 billion. Even smaller deepwater discoveries are easily worth $1 billion. Owning 20 percent of such a discovery results in an oil company obtaining a return equal to multiples of its risked investment—even when taking the other failures into account. These types of risk–reward calculations lead to the division of exploration risk among different owners. In doing so, a company and its investors decrease their upside but also substantially decrease the probability of complete failure.

The second factor that drives partnership is capital expenditure. The petroleum industry is subject to extraordinary capital demands. As mentioned, individual wells may exceed $100 million and the costs of developing a petroleum field can quickly soar into the billions before a barrel of oil is ever sold. This makes financing a constant challenge. Even after a discovery, companies may sell parts of their interests and bring in new partners to mitigate the capital challenges of development.

Risk mitigation can also interact with sunk capital costs in a project that has already been developed and is currently producing. The capital investments in production and transportation infrastructure and the value of the reserves in the ground are often sunk and immovable. Natural disasters or political events can threaten billions of dollars' worth of assets overnight. To mitigate this type of portfolio risk, companies often seek to have their assets spread across a geographically and politically diverse landscape rather than concentrated in one nation or area. Partnership facilitates this, as a company may prefer to own 20 percent of five different oil fields spread around the world rather than all of one.

Even if a company wished to own 100 percent of an international project, the host government may force it to share the project with other companies. The so-called "forced marriage" approach to petroleum projects is common in the developing world, where the government will seek to share the most attractive petroleum licenses so as to entice as many major oil companies as possible to invest in its petroleum sector. Developing nations may favor specific companies because of their reputations or technical capabilities, or others because of their country of origin (which can facilitate and cement relationships with other governments).

Just as a company can experience concentration risk from placing all of its investments in one country, so too can a country be exposed to concentration risk if its petroleum investment is primarily dominated by one international oil company. What if the organization decides to leave the region or country or goes bankrupt? Such a scenario could be harmful to the country's operations or its development and exploration plans. Its state oil company may not have the technical expertise to carry on the existing operations and it is unlikely to have access the same levels of capital for purposes of financing exploration and development.

The introduction of multiple international companies also advances competition for unlicensed resources. Once a developer is participating in one project, it will likely consider other projects, which may enable the host government to play the companies against each other to obtain higher bonuses and better commercial terms on its future oil and gas developments. The competition between companies can lead to competition among nations, as well, with oil companies from countries such as China and India competing for access to resources.

Finally, host governments may benefit from a diversity of perspective. The introduction of several international oil companies as partners in a project may enable officials to solicit and receive several views regarding how a project should be developed and operated. The competition of proposals may make it less likely that a government will make a really bad choice, as the presence of multiple companies serves as a check and balance on the decision-making process.

To Operate or Not?

If only one company owns a petroleum project, that company is the sole operator. This single company will be responsible for making the principal decisions relating to the development, budget creation, and funding of the operation. Its concern will be its rights and obligations opposite the host government.

The commercial structure becomes much more complex as the foreign contractor introduces one or more joint venture partners. This adds a new layer of decision making to the development. Before any proposal can be discussed with the host government, all foreign contractors will need to reach agreement. Differences of opinion on where a well should be drilled, the design for the well, how a development plan should proceed, and amounts of expenditures can slow down the decision-making process.

The joint operating agreement seeks to mitigate the potential for gridlock by appointing one of the contractors as the leader or operator.

The operator is charged with leading the internal approval process by initiating the proposals for petroleum activities, submitting them to the partnership group for approval, obtaining the government's approval, and, finally, executing the work program on the ground or at sea. If the partnership group cannot reach agreement on competing proposals, the joint operating agreement may give the operator's proposals a tiebreaker preference, thereby enabling the operator to break an impasse and continue any operations required by contracts with the government.

The operator usually conducts all joint operations on a no-gain and no-loss basis. This means that the party acting as the operator is not supposed to profit from the position of operator but merely recover its costs on a pass-through basis. The cost-recovery mechanisms of joint operating agreements include a pro rata sharing of all direct costs as well as a pro rata sharing of indirect costs, which are usually billed to the joint venture as a percentage of expenditures. The indirect costs reflect the overhead of the operator's other offices and personnel who participate from time to time on the project but whose time and expense is not directly allocated. For example, if $100 million is spent on petroleum costs over the course of a year, the operator might receive an overhead allocation of 3 percent of the first $20 million, 2 percent of the next $30 million, and 1 percent thereafter, for an annual overhead allocation of $1.7 million.

At these levels, it may be the case that companies view the role of operator as more economically burdensome than rewarding. As a company operates more properties, it must maintain greater overhead costs of many technical employees capable of conducting the petroleum extraction function. Overhead reimbursements may be insufficient to adequately cover the firm's cost of being an operator.

Operators face additional risks, as well. For example, the extraction function exposes operators to blowouts. In a particularly bad incident, such as an environmental catastrophe, nonoperators may refuse to contribute their share of costs pending litigation or arbitration over the operator's supervisory process and decisions. Joint operating agreements may impose liability on the operator for the gross negligence or willful misconduct of its supervisory personnel. Governments or third-party litigants may also focus their claims on the operator.

Even if the economic result is ultimately proportional liability, the media may target the operator. Headlines and breaking news stories that display the operator's logo, name, and personnel in the midst of a disaster can harm its reputation. Americans can easily name BP as the operator in the Deepwater Horizon oil spill, but how many can name the two nonoperators, Anadarko and Mitsui?

There is also the question of the relationship with the host government. The operator is viewed as the responsible party by the host government. In a disaster, or even in a dispute, the operator's relationship with the host government could be jeopardized. This can affect not only the economics of the particular project but also any other investments that company has in the same country. The operator could lose its licenses in the country and be precluded from participating in future petroleum investments. In contrast, nonoperators can often lay low and (privately) blame the operator.

Although both operators and nonoperators must comply with the Foreign Corrupt Practices Act (FCPA), the operator can be more exposed to potential FCPA situations. The operator is responsible for moving equipment into and out of the host country through customs. It negotiates various permits with the host government and employs consultants and others in the host country who may themselves engage in illegal activities.

Personnel issues can also influence a company's decision to operate. International operations require deployment of significant numbers of highly skilled personnel who generally must possess experience and interest in living abroad. Even in large companies, the number of personnel ready to be deployed to a remote international location may be limited. Only so many new international projects can be undertaken at once. Although expatriate compensation packages pay employees multiples of what they could earn in the United States, working spouses, family, and educational issues may render much of the home workforce unavailable for international deployment. There may also be concerns about safety in certain locations. Tropical diseases (such as malaria), high crime, kidnappings, terrorism, and other threats may discourage relocation.

One of the author's colleagues in Yemen

As a consequence, even large companies may adopt a nonoperated strategy on some portion of their international business development. This can enable a company to have the economic exposure of international operations without some of the risks that go with it. The nonoperated international strategy requires a business developer to carefully screen opportunities for two additional issues: operator quality and operator control issues.

Suppose a company has found a petroleum block that has an attractive prospect in which it would like to participate. If the company is unwilling to operate the block, it must decide if the current operator is acceptable. Operator considerations may include whether the company has the technical expertise and experience to operate the kind of wells required by the block. For example, if the block is in deepwater, does the current operator have sufficient deepwater experience? How has the company performed in its prior wells? Has it encountered any operational problems? Further,

U.S. companies will need to conduct due diligence on the operator from an ethical business conduct perspective to ensure that it has not engaged in past violations of the FCPA.

Operator control issues may also arise. If there is an existing joint operating agreement among the current owners, what minority protections are included in the document? What percentage of the owners must approve of different kinds of decisions? What happens in the event that the approval threshold cannot be reached? Does the joint operating agreement require the operator to submit authorizations for expenditure to the nonoperators for approval?

These issues of operator versus nonoperator control are generally less important in the international arena due to the regulatory oversight of the host government. The host government will audit and otherwise police the operator's expenditures through its own approval processes under the production sharing contract or local petroleum law. International nonoperators benefit from these requirements and are generally better protected from operator abuses than would be a similarly situated company in a U.S. lease.

THE JOINT OPERATING COMPANY

An alternative operating structure creates a new company, or joint operating company, that is responsible for operating the energy project. Figure 7.1 illustrates this approach. Each of the parties to the project owns its pro rata share of the joint operating company. The new company is usually named after the project and is staffed by equal numbers of personnel who are seconded to the operating company by the owners of the participating organizations. Joint operating companies can serve to resolve disputes when two companies both insist on operating. They can also mitigate quality or control issues if a new company entering the block is dissatisfied with the current operator or the control it wields under the joint operating agreement.

Figure 7.1: Individual Operator versus Joint Operating Company Approaches

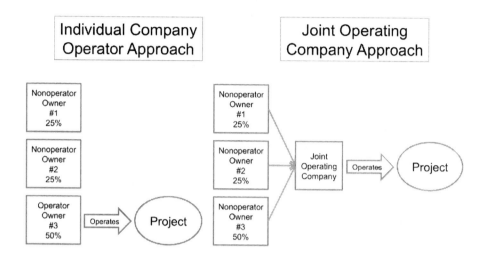

THE JOINT OPERATING AGREEMENT

Business developers working in the international arena often utilize the Association of International Petroleum Negotiators' (AIPN) joint operating agreement (JOA). Even when oil and gas companies have their own operating agreement template, it is usually based on the AIPN JOA. While the joint operating agreement is a complex document that often spans one hundred or more pages, it is useful to discuss some of its principal commercial terms.

- *Management of joint operations.* Whether the operator is an individual company or a specially created joint operations company, the JOA will have provisions prescribing the oversight of the operator by the project owners. Typically, oversight is accomplished though a committee made up of representatives nominated by the owners. Each representative is entitled to a vote equal to its company's ownership percentage.

- *Voting decisions.* The JOA specifies the percentage of votes required to approve certain matters before the operating committee. Higher percentage voting thresholds (supermajorities) are usually required for important decisions such as approval of development plans and annual work programs and budgets. A voting decision may require both a percentage threshold and the support of a specified number of companies. For example, certain votes may require the support of 65 percent of the owners with at least three owners voting in the affirmative. If Company A owns 40 percent, Company B owns 25 percent, Company C owns 15 percent, Company D owns 10 percent, and Company E owns 10 percent, Companies A and B would need at least one of the other owners to join them even though they control 65 percent of the votes. What happens if the owners are unable to agree to meet the voting pass mark? Joint operating agreements may provide for approvals by less than the required approval pass mark, or, in the case of a tie, the proposal favored by the operator may prevail.
- *Annual work program and budget.* One of the most contentious aspects of joint operations can be the approval of the annual work program and budget. On an annual basis, the operator proposes the work that will be undertaken in the coming year and its cost. Examples of disagreements include
  - ➤ Nonoperating owners may believe that the operator's proposed budget expenditures are unreasonable in terms of spending on employees, office space, or the operations themselves.
  - ➤ If seismic operations are included in the work program, owners may disagree about how much 2D or 3D is necessary or precisely where the seismic lines should be shot.
  - ➤ If well expenditures are included, owners may disagree on well location, well depth, well design, or the cost of the proposed drilling contract.
- *Authorizations for expenditures (AFE).* Most JOAs require that the operator submit AFEs over the course of the year, which

describe in more detail (than the annual work program and budget) the projects being undertaken and their cost. The AIPN model provides for three alternative AFE processes. Pursuant to the informational purposes only process (which is favored by operators), once an expenditure is approved in a budget, the details are submitted to the nonoperators as an AFE. No approval is required. Pursuant to the approval approach, large expenditures must be submitted to the parties in the form of an AFE that requires their approval before those expenditures can be made. This essentially creates a system of two votes on significant expenditures: at the annual work program and budget stage and at the AFE stage. Practically speaking, it is often the case that well locations and well designs are not yet complete at the time of the annual work program and budget. Thus, the AFE approval gives the nonoperators a chance to see the details before they make an expenditure decision. A third option is a hybrid of the two, which allows approval to be withheld for certain limited reasons. Among the reasons are inconsistency with the work program and budget, the proposed amount exceeding fair market cost, or a technical objection to the work being undertaken. Although an operator may prefer the informational purpose approach, it can result in more contentious annual budget meetings because the nonoperators will require more information about expenditures, technical designs of wells and facilities, and other matters before giving their annual budgetary approval.

- *Sole risk operations.* What happens if the party or parties wishing to pursue an optional operation (i.e., one that is not required under the minimum work program in the contract with the government) cannot get enough support from the others to conduct the project jointly? This is resolved by a provision in the JOA called sole risk that allows for some of the parties to undertake operations without the others. Under a sole-risk operation, the operator drills the well or shoots the seismic, but only the sole-risk minority parties pay for the operation. If the operation is successful and the nonparticipants wish to join at a later date, there is typically an opportunity to do so—but at a premium reflecting the fact that nonparticipants did not bear the risk of its failure. The nonparticipants are usually required to pay a significant cost, typically several times the expenditure they would have otherwise paid had they been a participating party.

- *Operator liability.* One contentious question under joint operating agreements is under what circumstances the operator can be disproportionately liable for losses. Generally, the AIPN approach is to limit the operator's liability to circumstances related to the gross negligence or willful misconduct of an operator's senior supervisory personnel. Gross negligence is generally defined as acting in reckless disregard of or wanton indifference to harmful consequences. Senior supervisory personnel can be defined at different levels, from a field supervisor to the project's general manager. Even if these thresholds are met, there may be additional limits on the amount of damages for which the operator is liable, such as replacement of damaged joint property or a hard-dollar ceiling on the total damages.

- *Cash calls and default.* The joint operating agreement contains detailed procedures for accounting and the collection of each party's share of costs. Practically speaking, once a work program and budget is approved, the operator sends cash calls to each of the owners that reflect each owner's percentage of upcoming costs. What happens when one of the owners does not pay? Others are required to pay their proportionate share of the defaulting owner's obligation. After all, the project must continue. If there are any profit distributions, the nonpaying owner's share is used to pay back the other owners (along with interest). Other AIPN remedies for nonpayment include (1) forfeiture, whereby the paying partners can require that any nonpaying owner forfeit its interest; and (2) buyout, pursuant to which the paying partners can purchase the nonpaying owner's interest at an appraised value.

Conclusion

Most petroleum assets are developed through the collaboration of several different companies that share costs, risks, work, and experience. One of these companies (or in some cases, a special purpose company) is appointed the operator. The operator and nonoperator(s) organize their activities under the framework of a joint operating agreement, which provides detailed procedures for decision making and management of the energy project. The principal advantage of being the operator is the ability to wield greater control over decisions. Nonoperators surrender some control in exchange for less risk, but the loss of control is largely mitigated by the host government's approval of significant matters. The economic values of an operating interest and a nonoperating interest in the same international project should be about the same because the operator conducts joint operations on a no-profit and no-loss basis.

CHAPTER 8

THE ACQUISITION PROCESS

C ompanies may acquire energy projects directly from foreign governments or secondhand through an existing owner. Primary acquisitions are undertaken by approaching the government and making offers for open or available concessions or by participating in government-run auctions. Secondary acquisitions entail acquiring the interest from an existing owner through a farm-in agreement, asset purchase agreement, or stock purchase agreement. Secondary acquisitions tend to be more expensive as they reflect a price premium for the value of the work undertaken by the current owner, including the primary acquisition itself.

PRIMARY ACQUISITIONS

Primary acquisitions can be open acreage or an interest that has reverted back to the government. In the case of open acreage, the geographic area in question (whether or not previously licensed to another company) is owned entirely by the government. No other company has any rights to the area, and whatever the acquiring company negotiates with the government will dictate not only that company's rights and obligations but also those of any later-comers. In the case of reversions, the acquiring company usually must accept the rights and obligations that exist under the past agreements. Reversions of interest can occur as a consequence of default, the exercise of the government's preferential purchase rights, or a company simply withdrawing from a project and returning its interest to the government.

Either type of interest may be acquired from the government in one of two ways: direct negotiation or competitive bidding.

- *Direct negotiation.* Direct negotiation is the preferable approach to acquiring petroleum interests from a government. The company approaches the government and proposes to acquire a concession pursuant to certain rights and obligations. The government then engages in a one-on-one negotiation with the company until terms are resolved and contracts are signed. A negative aspect of direct negotiation is the risk that the government will use a company's proposals and negotiating position as a stalking horse for obtaining better terms from other organizations. One way to discourage this practice is to execute a binding heads of agreement early in the negotiation process that sets forth an understanding between the parties regarding the principal terms and conditions of the transaction and provides for a period of exclusivity within which to conclude a transaction. If the government is unable to execute such a document in advance of the final production sharing agreement, it is still important to obtain verbal agreement that there is exclusivity and that the government will not engage in negotiations with other companies.

- *Competitive bidding.* Some governments prefer to license energy projects through an auction process. This can result in advantages for the government because it may encourage competition for the projects and perhaps higher bonuses. If a company knows that it only has one opportunity to win a project and that other companies may outbid it, the company is more likely to lead with its best price. In contrast, during a prolonged direct negotiation, a company may be able to start low and obtain better terms. A second advantage for the government is transparency and less risk of corruption. To the extent that bids in an auction are publicly opened and transparent, there is less risk of individual government officials making block awards (or specific contractual terms) contingent on personal bribes.

Secondary Acquisitions

Secondary acquisitions entail the buyer joining a contractual arrangement with the government that was negotiated by another company, perhaps many years in the past. This contract may or may not be better than what the acquiring company could negotiate directly with the government given current commodity prices and the history of success or failure of other projects in the region. For example, it is often the case that the percentage of a project that the government takes through participation and taxes increases over time as the number of petroleum discoveries in that nation increase. This is in part because the government may become less reliant on new projects due to cash inflows from existing projects.

There is also an element of the global marketplace for petroleum concessions at work in secondary acquisitions. International energy companies that are in competition for projects will flock to those areas where the chance of success is highest. This causes the price being offered by governments to rise and the fiscal terms for exploring companies to deteriorate. In such cases, older contracts for secondary acquisitions may have better terms than newer, primary contracts.

INTERNATIONAL ENERGY DEVELOPMENT

There are three basic agreements by which a company can acquire secondary rights in an energy project: (1) farm-in agreements; (2) asset purchase agreements; or (3) stock purchase agreements.

- *Farm-in agreements.* The most common arrangement whereby a company acquires rights to an energy project is a farm-in agreement. These agreements essentially bifurcate an existing interest in an energy project between two companies. For example, suppose Company A owns 100 percent of an energy project and Company B wishes to acquire 50 percent. This is usually accomplished through a farm-in agreement. The farm-in agreement will include a pro rata assignment to the buyer of all of the rights and obligations in the government contracts. The government must approve the assignment and accept the buyer as a substitute party for this portion of the seller's rights and obligations. If there are other company parties in the concession, they may also have to accept and approve the buyer in a similar fashion. Additionally, the farm-in agreement will usually contain negotiated terms between the seller and the buyer that neither affect the government nor any other company parties. For example, the agreement might require the buyer to pay its pro rata share of past costs that have been incurred in the project (as if it had been involved with the project from its inception) and to pay a "carry" of some future costs to the benefit of the seller (as consideration for the past risk assumed by the seller and the value that has been added over time). Posit the case where a well is about to be drilled. The buyer may commit to pay for not only its share of the next well being drilled, but also a portion of the seller's costs for the next well. Typical percentages of well carry amounts for farm-in agreements range from one and a quarter to two times the buyer's share of costs. If a buyer has a 20 percent interest in a $100-million well, its own share of costs would be $20 million. Thus, a one and a quarter carry would require the buyer to pay on behalf of the seller an additional $5 million (for $25 million total). A two times carry would require the buyer to pay on behalf of the seller an additional $20 million (for $40 million total). Should the buyer not meet these obligations, its interest is typically forfeited back to the seller.

- *Asset purchase agreement.* In cases where an owner is selling all of its interest in a project, the transaction is documented with an asset purchase agreement. Unlike a farm-in agreement, which may have continuing obligations, the asset purchase agreement generally provides for a fixed amount of consideration to be paid for the asset at a specific time and place. When the consideration is paid, the asset (or interest in the energy project) is transferred to the buyer simultaneously. Prior to the closing of an asset purchase agreement, the buyer will need to have concluded all title work and due diligence on the asset and to have obtained approvals from the government and any necessary other parties. After price, the negotiation for an asset sale and purchase agreement will focus on the seller's representations and warranties regarding that asset. The buyer will typically want representations and warranties regarding matters such as (1) marketable title, (2) good condition of the asset, (3) absence of pending or threatened litigation, (4) validity and enforceability of all concession rights, (5) appropriate corporate authorization of the sale, (6) accuracy of financial information provided to buyer, (7) reporting and payment of tax obligations, (8) compliance with laws, including the Foreign Corrupt Practices Act, (9) absence of environmental issues, and (10) no undisclosed liabilities. The seller should indemnify the buyer for any liability that originates from claims preceding the closing date.
- *Stock purchase agreement.* Energy assets are usually held in a special purpose company that has no other assets or business. This enables a company to farm in or acquire the asset indirectly through the acquisition of stock. For example, a company wishing to acquire a 10 percent interest from a seller that owns a 30 percent interest could either (1) buy the 10 percent interest directly through a farm-in or asset purchase agreement, or (2) acquire one-third of the stock in

the company that owns the 30 percent interest. Transactions of less than half of the stock of a company do not typically require government approval because there is no change of control over the underlying asset. It is also possible for the buyer to acquire all of the company's stock, which essentially transfers all underlying assets. Above the special purpose entities, there is usually a holding company for the country or region that owns several subsidiary (special purpose) organizations. If a company has multiple assets in a nation and is exiting the country altogether, the easiest way to effect the transaction may be to transfer the shares in the second-level holding company. Stock transactions require representations and warranties along the lines we have discussed as well as others that are specifically applicable to stock sales. As companies are legal entities that sign contracts, there is always the possibility that a company being acquired has some hidden liability that was not disclosed or ascertainable beforehand. Assuming that the seller is a creditworthy company, this risk is mitigated through the seller's indemnification of the buyer for any liability that might arise before the closing takes place.

COMPARING PRIMARY AND SECONDARY ACQUISITIONS

Business developers may encounter the issue of whether an acquisition strategy should focus on primary or secondary acquisitions or be indifferent between the two. The government may resell some interests in existing projects, but most primary acquisitions are of open acreage. These areas are generally frontier with little prior exploration activity. This means that primary acquisitions tend to be higher risk when compared with secondary acquisitions. It also means they tend to be lower in cost.

Another advantage of primary acquisitions is that the company initially contracting with the government is able to negotiate the terms and conditions and receive 100 percent of the interest in the project. By owning 100 percent of the interest, the company can resell portions of the project to other organizations through farm-in arrangements. Such efforts can result in the buyer paying all or most of the exploration costs to the seller, at least for a period of time.

Primary acquisitions generally involve energy projects that are at their earliest point in a project lifecycle. They may be five or more years away from initial cash flow. Many companies prefer secondary acquisitions for the opportunity to acquire projects with existing cash flow or projects that are closer to the realization of cash flow. Projects without cash flows are harder to finance due to their higher risk and the inability to make interest payments on a debt facility. A company can accelerate its growth by acquiring later-life projects through secondary acquisition.

One of my companies studied the optimal timing for exploration project entry and found that the best economic point of entry is immediately before the first exploration well. At this point, the prior owners have acquired 2D seismic, identified prospects and then shot 3D seismic over the best of them. The risk-assessment teams of one or more other companies have thoroughly analyzed all geological and geophysical data on the prospects and selected the best of these to be drilled. The fact that at least one other company is willing to place its capital at risk is a vote of confidence, and the better the company's reputation, the more valuable is its well approval.

At this same time, no well has penetrated petroleum, which means that there are no reserves to purchase. As such, farm-in costs remain tied to historical and future exploration costs rather than the discounted value of barrels of petroleum reserves. It is at this point that a company can pay perhaps two times its share of an individual well and turn that investment into hundreds of millions to billions of dollars. The chance of success will be perhaps one in five, one in four, or one in three. No casino would allow a gambler to obtain a return of many tens of multiples with such high odds of success. It is this disproportionate return at the moment of the first well that well-funded exploration companies focus on.

Secondary acquisitions may be easier to acquire from a purely transactional perspective. The counterparty is typically another international energy company that has a corporate decision-making and negotiation process. Such companies will negotiate a binding letter of intent or heads of agreement that sets forth the principal commercial terms. They will agree to provide the buyer with a period of exclusivity within which to close the transaction. These agreements often contain standstill clauses that prohibit the seller from soliciting, encouraging, or engaging in any discussion with other potential buyers. International energy companies view time as valuable and are likely to seek to close a transaction as quickly as possible, usually in a couple of months.

Primary acquisitions with governments tend to take longer to complete—typically six months to a year. One reason is that government negotiators may not have sufficient discretion and may have to periodically adjourn negotiations to consult with the minister. Final government approvals may even require an act of Parliament or a decree from the head of state.

The different incentives of governments and private companies also may lead to swifter negotiations among private companies. International oil companies are likely to run into each other frequently, and negotiators have personal reputations at stake. This creates an incentive for cooperation, consistency, and honesty in negotiations. Companies may have model agreements (or positions on issues) that differ little whether they are sellers or buyers, thereby narrowing the number of issues being negotiated. In contrast, governments may not view any individual company as particularly important and may pit one company against another. All of this means that several secondary transactions may be concluded in the same amount of time as it takes to close a single primary one.

Conclusion

The acquisition process typically follows one of two paths: primary acquisition directly from the government or secondary acquisition from existing owners of energy assets. Each of these paths has a different structure under which energy assets may be acquired.

Primary acquisitions are made through a direct negotiation with the host government or via a competitive bidding round or auction. Secondary acquisitions can be structured as farm-in agreements, asset sales, or stock sales, depending on the goals of the seller and buyer. While there are advantages and disadvantages to each approach, secondary acquisitions tend to be easier to conclude and lower risk but come with a steeper price tag.

CHAPTER 9

STRUCTURING UPSTREAM PROJECTS

O ne of the principal responsibilities of a business developer is structuring transactions. A developer needs to understand the types of commercial arrangements that exist with governments around the world. How does the host government tax the project? How much of the petroleum revenue will the company receive, and in what years? Whether a company enters a project through a primary transaction or a secondary transaction, the government's fiscal regime will have an impact on project profitability. The approaches of different nations vary, but there are three main types of upstream fiscal regimes: (1) production sharing contracts; (2) tax and royalty regimes; and (3) service agreements.

PRODUCTION SHARING CONTRACTS

Production sharing contracts are the most common type of fiscal regime encountered around the world. At its simplest, an international energy company receives reimbursement of its costs of exploration, development, and operation, and the remaining cash flow cascades into a formula that divides net revenue between the international energy company and the host government. In other words, the production (net of costs) is shared between the foreign partner and the host government.

How much of the production can be used for recovery of costs is a negotiated term. In petroleum developments, the cost recovery pool can run into the many billions of dollars before the first barrel of oil is ever produced. It may take several years of production just to reimburse the contractor group for development costs. As such, a government may impose a ceiling on the amount of oil that can be used for cost recovery in any one year. This helps to ensure that at least some of the production will flow to the government as profit. Usually, something on the order of two-thirds to four-fifths of production is available for cost recovery.

Figure 9.1 shows how the production sharing agreement (PSA) is structured in a three-company petroleum concession.

Figure 9.1: Production Sharing Agreement

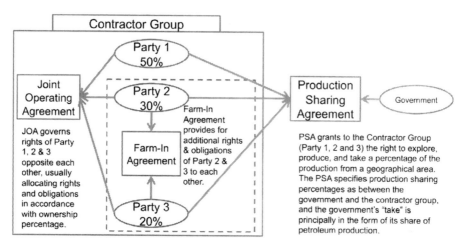

The following example demonstrates how the production-sharing regime works:

- The contractor group produces 100,000 barrels of oil, which have been sold at $50 per barrel for total revenues of $5,000,000.
- The contractor group's costs, including past capital and operating costs, are $1,000,000.
- The production sharing agreement specifies that the contractor group keep the number of barrels equal to its costs *plus* 35 percent of the remaining barrels (i.e., the profit oil).
- As such, the contractor group keeps proceeds equal to $1,000,000 for cost oil (20,000 barrels) *plus* $1,400,000 for profit oil (28,000 barrels).
- These amounts are divided among the parties in the contractor group in accordance with their participating interests.
- The government keeps the remainder of the oil (i.e., 65 percent of the profit oil, or $2,600,000).

Figure 9.2 illustrates how revenues flow under a production sharing agreement regime. Note that the profit oil percentage (or government take) tends to increase with the success of prospects in a block or nation. In rich petroleum reservoirs such as offshore Angola and Nigeria, the profit sharing percentages are substantially weighted in favor of the government.

Figure 9.2: Cascade of Revenues in Production Sharing Agreement

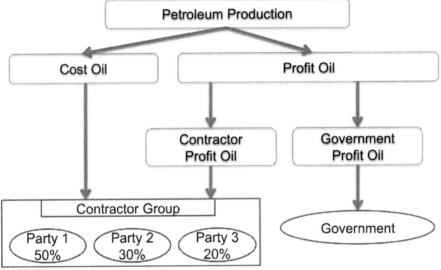

Most production sharing agreements contain considerably more complex calculations for how much oil flows to the international energy companies versus the government. Some examples of these approaches include

- *Rate of Production.* The percentage of profit oil flowing to the international oil company will be higher for the initial barrels produced and then reduced as production quantities increase. For example, the profit oil from the first 10,000 barrels per day of production might be divided so that 70 percent flows to the contractor and 30 percent flows to the government, whereas any production over 100,000 barrels per day may be divided in the reverse direction, with 70 percent flowing to the government and 30 percent to the contractor group. Amounts in between may be divided on a sliding scale.

- *R-Factors.* Governments can also allocate profit oil based on accrued net earnings divided by accrued total expenditures. This is referred to as an R-Factor. During the exploration and development phases of an energy project, the R-Factor is zero because there are no net earnings and increasing amounts of expenditures. Once production starts, the top line of the R-Factor gradually grows in size and at some point should exceed the bottom line. This is essentially the break-even point, where dollars expended equal dollars earned. At this point, the R-Factor becomes one. Some R-Factors provide a cost of capital component to equalize for the time value of historical costs, as well. R-Factor–based contracts typically weight petroleum sharing strongly in favor of the international energy company until the R-Factor exceeds one. The growth of the R-Factor over the life of a project is a measure of increasing profitability, and the government's share of production will rise along with it. Similarly, if revenues decline and costs increase, the R-Factor may decline, thereby leading to increased production sharing by the international energy company.

- *Rate of return.* A similar effect to the R-Factor approach can be achieved through rate-of-return production sharing tranches. As previously discussed, governments often view the production sharing contract as a quasiregulatory system to ensure that the companies developing its resources do not receive excessive returns on their investments. Rate-of-return tranches can provide governments assurance that if circumstances such as high oil prices result in the project being much more profitable than anticipated, most of the excess profits will flow to the government. Similarly, a formula that allocates to the company increasing amounts of petroleum when its rate of return is low can help soften the impact of low commodity prices or high project costs.

Caspian oil field

TAX AND ROYALTY REGIMES

Tax and royalty regimes provide the host government with two sources of revenue: a royalty and an income tax. The provisions to establish the royalty and tax can be set forth in a contract (such as a concession agreement or exploration and production right) or in regulations or statutes.

A royalty is a share of gross revenues taken off the top line, irrespective of costs. In this type of fiscal regime, the host government will immediately receive a share of production revenue, which can be advantageous because it tends to smooth the government's cash flow from a project. In contrast, production sharing agreements can be more back-end loaded for governments. A government may receive little revenues from a production sharing agreement during the early years of a project because the contractor must recover billions of dollars in development costs. This decreases the amount of profit oil. Political frustration can build under a production sharing contract when a government has to wait many years to materially share in project revenues. Royalties can help keep the host government content by providing an immediate cash flow.

After the government has received its royalty, the balance of the revenues flow through an income tax mechanism that allows deductions for petroleum costs. The after-tax income is then distributed to each member of the contractor group. Income tax rates are usually similar to the highest marginal corporate tax rate in the United States. This is in part due to U.S. tax policy that allows for foreign tax credits. The use of income taxes as a mechanism for the government take (when compared with others of equal value) has potential benefits for U.S. companies because these tax payments are often creditable against the company's U.S. income taxes. Figure 9.3 illustrates the structure of a typical tax and royalty regime.

Figure 9.3: Tax and Royalty Regime

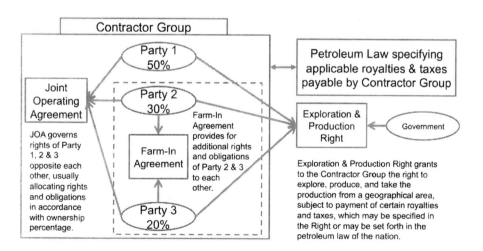

The following example demonstrates how the tax and royalty regime works:

- The contractor group produces 100,000 barrels of oil, which have been sold at $50 per barrel for total revenues of $5,000,000.
- The contractor group's costs, including past capital and operating costs, are $1,000,000.
- The exploration and production right specifies that the contractor group be subject to a 10 percent royalty based on gross production and a 35 percent income tax on net profits.
- The 10 percent royalty comes off the top, such that $500,000 is payable to the host government irrespective of whether any profit is made.
- After deduction of the contractor group's costs, a taxable profit of $3,500,000 remains ($5,000,000 - $500,000 royalty - $1,000,000).
- The contractor group then pays the government an income tax of $1,225,000 ($3,500,000 x 35 percent).
- Thus, the contractor group keeps gross proceeds equal to $3,275,000 ($5,000,000 - $500,000 royalty - $1,225,000 income tax), of which $1,000,000 represents its costs and $2,275,000 represents its after-tax profits.
- The government take equals the sum of the royalty and income tax, or $1,725,000.

This revenue cascade is shown in Figure 9.4.

Figure 9.4: Cascade of Revenues in a Tax and Royalty Regime

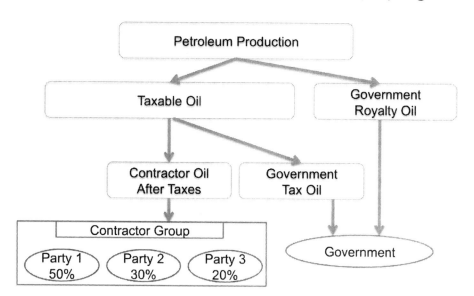

As with production sharing contracts, there can be formulaic mechanisms in the law or contracts that adjust the amount of the royalty or the tax rate based on factors such as production levels, the R-Factor, the rate of return, or whether a project is onshore, in shallow water, or in deepwater.

Further, fiscal regimes can incorporate characteristics of both production sharing contracts and tax and royalty regimes. Production sharing contracts can have, in addition to production sharing mechanisms, a royalty or an income tax (or both). Because of the complexity of fiscal regimes, the business developer must create an economic model for the project that shows the impact to the company's rate of return and net present value under different sets of assumptions. In a primary negotiation, a dynamic economic model can help the negotiating team understand the costs and benefits from making certain concessions or trades on fiscal terms.

SERVICE AGREEMENTS

The third primary class of fiscal regime is a service agreement. In service agreements, the international energy company is merely reimbursed its out-of-pocket costs and given a negotiated fee (representing profit) for executing the project. Service agreements are relatively rare in upstream businesses because the company usually does not have any entitlement to production and is therefore generally unable to book reserves. Figure 9.5 illustrates the commercial structure of a service agreement.

Figure 9.5: Service Agreement Regime

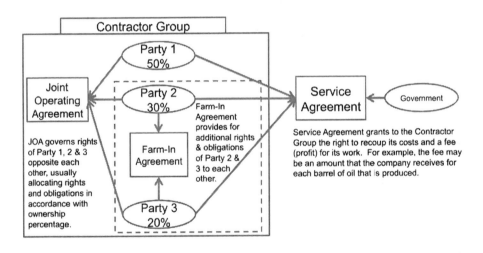

The following example demonstrates how the service agreement regime works:

- The contractor group produces 100,000 barrels of oil, which have been sold at $50 per barrel for total revenues of $5,000,000.
- The contractor group's costs, including past capital and operating costs, are $1,000,000.

- The service agreement specifies that the contractor group be paid its costs plus a fee (or profit) of $5 per barrel.
- Thus, the contractor group's payment under the service agreement is $1,000,000 for the costs it incurred and $500,000 in profits.
- The host government's take equals $3,500,000—the amount remaining after deduction of the contractor group's costs and service fee.

Figure 9.6 shows the revenue flow in a service agreement regime.

Figure 9.6: Cascade of Revenues in a Service Regime

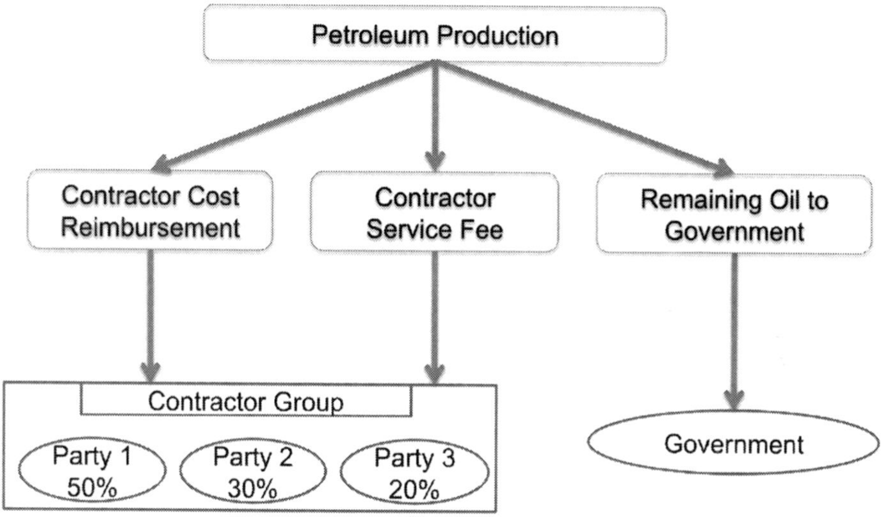

CONCLUSION

There are three principal fiscal regimes in the upstream energy sector: production sharing agreements, tax and royalty concessions, and service agreements. Over time, the distinctions between production sharing agreements and tax and royalty regimes have blurred as governments have incorporated a mix of the provisions under different contracts. While the economic result of any fiscal regime can be adjusted to provide the international energy company with about the same rate of return or net present value, different regimes may have different impacts on different companies. Some companies may value the ability to use foreign tax credits or book reserves more than others. Similarly, some companies may want to negotiate contracts that provide them with more upside potential while others may prefer structures that automatically adjust and protect them in the event of lower commodity prices or higher costs.

CHAPTER 10

STRUCTURING
PIPELINE PROJECTS

W hen oil production takes place offshore, tankers arrive by
sea and offload petroleum directly from the production
facilities. Onshore production of oil and gas raises
different issues because the petroleum must be transported from
where it is produced to a market. Offshore natural gas may also
need to be transported by pipeline to an onshore location, where
it can be used by a market or delivered to a liquefied natural gas
(LNG) facility. In such cases, a midstream pipeline project is
required to achieve commerciality. The owners of the project may
be the owners of the petroleum, entirely different companies, or a
mix of the two. The structures of pipeline projects usually consist
of pipeline development agreements that set forth the overall
rights among the consortium and the government as well as
either pipeline transportation agreements, pursuant to which the
consortium charges a tariff or fee to transport petroleum, or back-
to-back commodity sales contracts through which the consortium
purchases all of the petroleum at the start of the pipeline and then
resells it into the market.

PIPELINE DEVELOPMENT AGREEMENTS

In the midstream sector, international pipeline projects usually start with a consortium of companies that have stranded petroleum resources. These companies have been involved in an exploration project and have discovered oil or gas, but the location of the petroleum may be hundreds or even thousands of miles away from a market where it can be sold. The companies may join together in a joint venture through one or more agreements to construct the facilities required to transport the petroleum to a market. Other organizations with specific expertise in pipeline projects may also join the consortium. Together they seek to negotiate a pipeline development agreement that sets forth the rights and obligations of various parties and governments in the pipeline project.

One of the threshold issues for discussion is the allocation of capacity on the pipeline. Will the pipeline be large enough to be able to accommodate all of the producers' capacity? If so, the allocation is a product of calculating each producer's share of the regional production that will be shipped on the pipeline. Even then, there can be issues surrounding the technical realities of timing for when different producers will achieve their peak production, how long production will last from different fields, and the decline curves associated with individual production areas. As such, pipeline ownership percentages are unlikely to be an exact match for the needs of each producer over time, and circumstances may change over twenty or thirty years and result in some pipeline owners having insufficient capacity to ship their production and others having excess capacity.

Another issue that can arise is the commingling of petroleum streams from different fields. All oil and gas is not equally valuable. Oil values may be affected by various quality characteristics such as how light or heavy it is and how much sulfur or wax it contains. When different types of oil are delivered on a pipeline, they commingle, and the result at the pipeline outlet is a blended stream that may be more or less valuable than the oil delivered into the line by different producers. In order to compensate the producers of higher value petroleum (who deliver a barrel that is worth more than what they receive), pipelines have a contractual mechanism called a quality bank, which requires those producers of lower value petroleum to compensate (in barrels or cash) the producers of higher value petroleum.

Pipeline development agreements also may include government counterparties. If a pipeline is constructed entirely within one nation, the pipeline development agreement may only need the government's approval for establishment of its right-of-way. However, it is often the case that pipelines cross international borders. Cross-border pipelines create additional complications because not all nations on the pipeline right-of-way participate in the bounty of revenues from petroleum production.

Cross-border pipeline development agreements provide for the taxation of the transportation function among the various countries that fall along the pipeline's route. This is usually achieved through mileage allocation. Assume that a pipeline charges $5 per barrel to ship oil for five hundred miles across two nations. Country A accounts for one hundred miles of the pipeline's length and Country B accounts for four hundred miles. In this case, Country A would be able to tax $1 of revenue whereas Country B would be able to tax $4 of revenue.

Pipeline facility in Ecuador

Other development-related agreements may include

- Right-of-way agreements across government and private lands
- A cross-border cooperation treaty among each of the nations regarding the pipeline interconnection
- A joint operating agreement among the owners of the pipeline consortium for purposes of creating a pipeline management company and dividing costs and revenues
- A project finance agreement among the pipeline consortium and one or more banks concerning debt financing of the project
- Engineering, procurement, and construction contracts among the pipeline consortium and the companies that will build the pipeline.

TARIFFS AND TRANSPORTATION AGREEMENTS

The U.S. energy industry is familiar with the tariff approach to pipeline transportation. The nation is crossed by many pipelines owned by companies that charge a toll per unit of petroleum for transportation between various points on the system. A similar approach can be taken with international pipeline projects.

Under the tariff or transportation agreement approach, the petroleum being shipped never becomes the property of the pipeline consortium. The producer of the petroleum is responsible for its market value and assumes any risk of resale value at the point of delivery. The pipeline consortium merely provides a transportation service, and the owner of the petroleum pays a fee. Figure 10.1 illustrates this commercial structure.

Figure 10.1: Transportation Agreement Structure

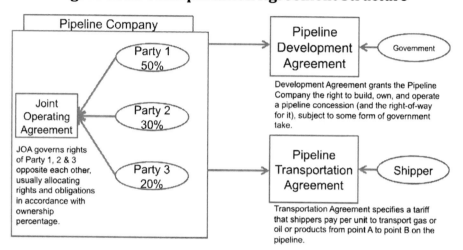

The principal difference between transportation arrangements in a mature market, such as the United States, and those in a developing world location is the requirement of long-term contracts (ship-or-pay) in international locations. The failure of any one producer to ship its petroleum on a pipeline in the United States is unlikely to have a material impact on a pipeline owner because there are many producers in the United States shipping to many suppliers. One shipper goes off the pipeline and another replaces it. In contrast, remote international pipelines may depend on the production from one or a few upstream petroleum developments. Before a pipeline can be financed (either through corporate capital or debt), there will need to be long-term transportation agreements in place that guarantee a minimum cash flow to the pipeline owners for a long enough period to ensure that the cost of constructing the pipeline is recouped along with a reasonable rate of return. Such ship-or-pay arrangements require the owners of petroleum to ship a minimum quantity of petroleum or, if the minimum is not reached, to pay the tariff as if the petroleum had been shipped.

BACK-TO-BACK PURCHASE AGREEMENTS

The back-to-back purchase agreement approach entails more risk for the pipeline consortium than merely charging petroleum shippers a tariff. Under this approach, the pipeline consortium agrees to purchase the commodity at the start of the pipeline. It becomes the owner of the petroleum and has title to it until it is resold to a buyer at the end of the pipeline. If petroleum is purchased but cannot be resold at a higher price, the pipeline consortium suffers a loss. To the extent that it can be sold for a higher price, the consortium retains the difference as revenue.

Practically speaking, this market risk is mitigated through back-to-back agreements, under which the consortium purchases petroleum at one end of the pipeline and simultaneously resells it. In the case of crude, the price mechanism is usually an index price based on a basket of similar petroleum. With respect to natural gas projects, price is more likely to be negotiated to reflect local market conditions rather than global averages. The purchase price will be lower than the sale price to reflect the cost of the transportation being provided. Essentially, the difference between the purchase price and the sale price is the tariff being charged to customers and is likely to be subject to annual inflation. The back-to-back approach is illustrated in Figure 10.2.

Figure 10.2: Back-to-Back Petroleum Sales Agreement Structure

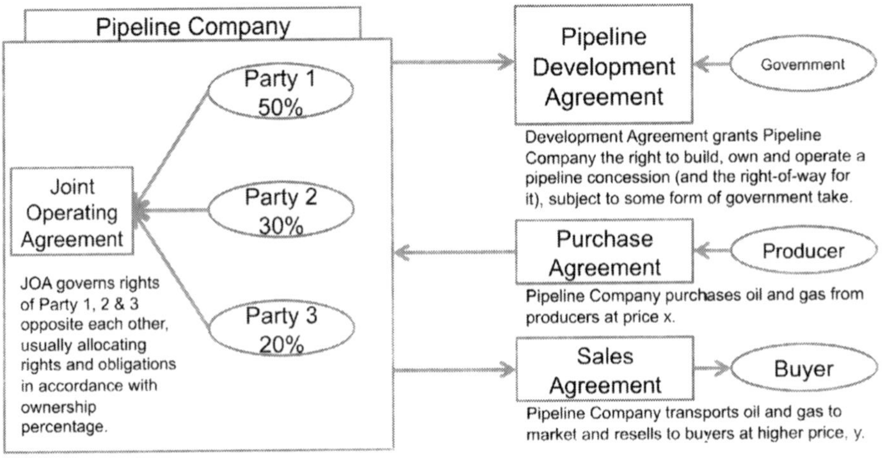

Most production purchases and sales need to be back-to-back in every respect. This means that the term of the contract must be for the same period of time. The quantity of petroleum purchased each day must be identical. And, most importantly, the obligation to purchase petroleum must be contingent on the ability to sell the petroleum downstream to buyers and the obligation to deliver petroleum must be contingent on the ability to purchase petroleum from the upstream project. In other words, there should never be a situation in which the pipeline consortium can be held liable for events at either end of the pipeline that are beyond its reasonable control. This is a force majeure (or suspension) concept. If the input or the output of the linked contracts is disrupted, the pipeline consortium simply passes the effect of the disruption on to the other, unaffected party(ies).

That being said, it may be advantageous for a gas pipeline consortium to de-link the price terms for perhaps 10 percent of the natural gas it purchases. This enables the sale of some portion of the natural gas at floating or spot market prices, which could be higher than the prices of a long-term contract. For example, there may be small industrial customers in the local gas market who are willing to pay a premium for access to natural gas because they are currently using alternative fuels like oil or diesel that cost significantly more than natural gas on an energy equivalent basis. In this type of structure, the pipeline consortium would be assuming the risk that the resale price for 10 percent of its gas might be less than the purchase price.

Would the upside potential be worth the assumption of risk? Suppose long-term natural gas is purchased for $2 and sold into market at $3 (mostly to government gas-fired power plants), with perhaps $0.75 of the differential being cost recovery and $0.25 representing the profit to the pipeline consortium investors. In the same market, there might be an industrial park next to a gas-fired power plant filled with energy consumers such as auto parts and porcelain manufacturers who purchase spot diesel or fuel oil for an energy equivalent price of $10 or $12. None of these customers may be sufficiently creditworthy to purchase gas on a long-term basis, nor may these types of customers be willing to commit to purchases of natural gas for decades at a time. There also may be some incremental cost for these customers to switch fuel types or be linked into the pipeline network.

Even so, suppose that over time, 10 percent of the natural gas production is sold to small industrial customers at an average price of $8. For 10 percent of the natural gas being sold, the profit component for the pipeline consortium increases from $0.25 to $5.25. Such market-based pricing can double or triple the profitability of a gas project. Small portions of supply can be sold to buyers at premium prices and the overall profitability of the pipeline consortium can increase, but so does the risk that these quantities may not be sold.

CONCLUSION

Pipeline projects are typically structured with a development agreement that sets forth the rights and obligations of the pipeline's investors as well as any nations across which the pipeline will be constructed. This is equivalent to a concession or production sharing agreement in the upstream sector because it grants the basic rights to build, own, and operate a pipeline. Agreements must also be put in place concerning the long-term flow of petroleum through the pipeline. These arrangements take the form of either (1) tariff-based transportation agreements, under which the owners of petroleum commit to ship petroleum on the pipeline for several decades at specified prices, or (2) back-to-back purchase and sale agreements, pursuant to which the pipeline consortium simultaneously purchases petroleum from the owners of production and resells it into the market at the termination of the pipeline.

CHAPTER 11

STRUCTURING POWER PROJECTS

The ultimate buyers of petroleum from a pipeline project are often gas-fired electricity generation plants. Some are government-owned and others belong to energy companies. An energy company that discovers a large quantity of natural gas in a remote area may devise and construct a power project to convert gas that has no value into electricity that can be sold to consumers. As with pipelines, power projects commence with the host government granting the right to build, own, and operate an electricity plant. In conjunction with such development rights, the party constructing the plant typically enters into two sets of back-to-back agreements: (1) fuel supply agreements, pursuant to which it purchases the input (natural gas) to run the plant; and (2) power purchase agreements through which it sells the output (of electricity) created by the burning of natural gas.

POWER PROJECT DEVELOPMENTS

Power projects entail a suite of development agreements similar to those of a pipeline consortium. There is a concession agreement with the government of the host nation that sets forth the terms and conditions for the power project to construct, own, and operate the plant. This agreement will include grants for land and any right-of-ways required for fuel supply or power transmission lines. It may also address terms and conditions under which the government utility company can buy power from the plant. Other development-stage agreements include the operating agreement among the power consortium; project financing agreements with banks; and engineering, procurement, and construction agreements.

Dubai power plants

The host government's compensation may take the form of income tax on the project company or it may result from discounted electricity generation. If the government owns the electric utility in the nation and is purchasing all of the electricity from the power project, the principal negotiation between the power consortium and the government may be the price at which the government purchases electricity. These types of negotiations look very similar to utility cost-of-service regulation in the United States. The power consortium will need to demonstrate to the government, through the use of economic modeling, that the price at which the government is buying electricity is approximately equal to that amount necessary to enable the power consortium to recover the cost of constructing the power plant and related facilities, the cost of purchasing fuel, and a reasonable rate of return on its investment in the plant.

Power projects in some ways resemble the back-to-back commodity agreements in pipeline projects because the power consortium has to purchase a commodity at the input of the plant (fuel) and sell a commodity at the output of the plant (power). These agreements must be sufficiently aligned to avoid situations where the power consortium is left purchasing too much fuel at too high of a price relative to what it can sell electricity for as an output of the plant. Terms such as duration of the contract, force majeure, quantity, price, and type of currency (dollar versus local) must be carefully aligned to avoid liability to the power consortium for circumstances that are beyond its reasonable control. Figure 11.1 illustrates the structure of a power project.

Figure 11.1: Typical Structure of a Power Project

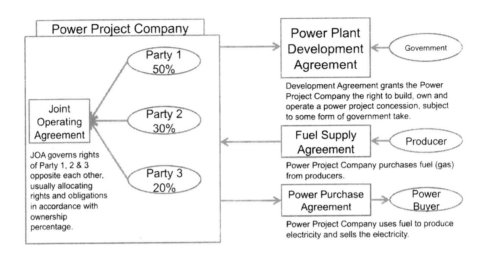

THE FUEL SUPPLY AGREEMENT: THE SELLER'S OBLIGATION TO DELIVER GAS

Parties to fuel supply agreements or gas sales and purchase agreements (GSPA) have created a wide array of contractual provisions to capture different types of delivery obligations on the part of the seller. In each case, though, the provisions must meet the power project's gas consumption needs without exceeding the seller's delivery capability. It is also important that the provisions not reserve more of the seller's production, processing, and transportation capacity than is reasonably necessary to meet the electricity plant's needs.

- *Annual contract quantity.* The annual contract quantity (ACQ) is the power project's annual entitlement to gas or, to put it another way, the maximum quantity of gas that the power project has a right to take during a year. The ACQ is usually expressed as a firm annual number in millions of standard cubic feet (mmscf) or billions of British Thermal Units (BTUs). A GSPA may have one ACQ that applies to every year of the contract or different ACQs applicable to different years. For example, if a power project's electricity market is growing, it might seek to increase the ACQ over time. The ACQ might decrease over time if the power project expects to replace less efficient facilities with more efficient facilities or if the gas seller anticipates that its gas production will decline over time.

- *Daily contract quantity.* The daily contract quantity (DCQ) represents the typical, or average, amount of gas that the power project expects to purchase on a given day under the GSPA. If the power project expects to purchase the same quantity every day of the year, the DCQ is usually expressed as the ACQ divided by 365. A power project's DCQ also can vary over the course of a year. For example, an electricity plant may consume more gas in the summer as a consequence of greater air-conditioning use by its customers. The GSPA addresses such variations by forecasting the power project's average gas consumption for each month and then specifying these figures as monthly DCQs in an appendix.

- *Maximum daily quantity.* The maximum daily quantity (MDQ) is the daily equivalent of the ACQ. It represents the *maximum* quantity that the power project has a right to take during a given day. The MDQ is expressed as a percentage (usually 105 percent to 120 percent) of the DCQ.

- *Additional gas.* One risk that the power project may wish to address in the GSPA is the possibility of exhausting the ACQ before the end of the year. The GSPA may provide for the power project to request quantities above the ACQ. This is referred to as additional gas. Additional gas usually has a higher price, perhaps 105 percent to 130 percent of the price of normal gas. While the seller is under no obligation to provide additional gas, the price premium provides it with an incentive to do so.

- *Bank gas.* Additional gas is only sold to the power project at the seller's discretion. Bank gas is a firm commitment from the seller to provide certain quantities of gas above the ACQ. Under such an arrangement, should the power project exceed the ACQ, the seller would be obligated to deliver an additional quantity of gas over the course of the year. The GSPA can also provide for bank gas when the MDQ is exceeded. In most cases, the quantity of bank gas available in a day or over several days will be limited by the engineering of the natural gas pipeline. When a producer commences production, the first shipments of gas pack the empty space in the pipeline, creating a kind of gas storage facility. Bank gas is usually provided from the line pack in a pipeline as gas buyers withdraw more gas from the pipeline than is being produced into it.

- *Seller-nominated GSPAs.* It is not always possible for the seller to know what quantities it will produce over the term of a GSPA. This can be the case with an associated gas field, where the quantity of gas is tied to crude oil production. Production uncertainty can also be the result of reservoir depletion. In such cases, the GSPA can address the seller's risk of committing to more gas than it may eventually be able to deliver by allowing the seller to specify its available quantities on a rolling basis (the seller-nominated GSPA). Under a seller-nominated GSPA, the DCQ is nominated a day or more in advance by the seller as the quantity that it is capable of delivering on that day. The ACQ under a seller-nominated GSPA is calculated by summing the seller's specified DCQs over the course of the year.

- *Total contract quantity.* Total contract quantity is the power project's entitlement to gas over the entire life of the GSPA—that is, the maximum quantity that the power project has a right to take during the term of the GSPA. The total contract quantity usually represents the amount of gas that can be withdrawn from the reservoir before the seller is uncertain of its capability to meet the ACQ and MDQ thresholds. When the total contract quantity is surpassed, the GSPA usually terminates. Alternatively, it may shift from a regime of enumerated DCQs to one of a seller-nominated GSPA.

- *Liquidated damages and guaranteed delivery quantities.* The consequences of a seller's failure to deliver a quantity that a power project is entitled to receive vary greatly. Some GSPAs provide that the seller's only penalty for delivery failure is a reduction in the power project's obligation to purchase gas. More typically, a GSPA dictates a liquidated damages credit or payment, which is usually expressed as a percentage of the gas price (e.g., 30 percent). For example, if the seller failed to deliver 100 mmscf, the next 100 mmscf delivered to the power project would be subject to a 30 percent discount. In such a case, the seller will usually seek to negotiate additional limits on the liquidated damages provision. One common provision is a maximum liability limitation that caps the seller's liquidated damages at a sum certain during any single year and over the entire term of the GSPA. Liquidated damages provisions may also be limited to the positive difference, if any, between the power project's cost of replacement fuel and the gas price. This protects the seller from a situation in which the power project incurs little or no actual damages.

THE FUEL SUPPLY AGREEMENT: THE POWER PROJECT'S OBLIGATION TO PURCHASE GAS

GSPAs typically provide for daily, monthly, and annual thresholds, which establish minimum revenues for the seller, irrespective of the power project's actual consumption. While the power project can take anything between zero and the maximum daily quantity on a given day, or between zero and the annual contract quantity during a year, there are usually economic penalties for taking too little gas. These penalties help the seller recover its investments in its production, processing, and transportation facilities.

- *Annual take or pay quantity.* The annual take or pay quantity is the minimum amount of gas that the power project must take and pay for over the course of the year. If, at the end of the year, the power project's off take is less than the annual take or pay quantity, the power project must pay the gas price for the quantity shortfall as if it had been taken. The annual take or pay quantity is usually between 80 percent and 95 percent of the ACQ.

- *Daily minimum quantity and monthly take or pay quantity.* In addition to annual minimum quantities, a power project may be required to purchase (whether actually used or not) minimum quantities of gas each day or each month. This can be due to the producer's or pipeline project's financing or other commercial requirements. For example, as gas is produced and processed in a plant, other products may be produced and sold to third parties. These may include ethane, propane, butane, or condensate. If the power plant does not take enough gas, less of these other products will be produced.

- *Make-up gas.* When a power project pays for gas that it does not consume, it usually receives a credit allowing it to take all or part of this gas in future years—either at a reduced price or for free. Before gaining the privilege of make-up gas, the power project must meet the take or pay quantity in a subsequent year.

- *Carry forward.* Power projects sometimes seek to have a subsequent year's take or pay percentage reduced by the amount that the power project exceeds the previous year's take or pay percentage. This arrangement is called a carry forward. For example, suppose the power project's take or pay percentage is 90 percent of the ACQ. In Year One, the power project consumes 100 percent of the ACQ. The difference of 10 percentage points (between what the power project took, 100 percent, and the take or pay percentage of 90 percent) is carried forward and deducted from the Year Two take or pay percentage so that the power project's take or pay percentage in Year Two is only 80 percent (90 percent - 10 percent).

THE POWER PURCHASE AGREEMENT: ALIGNING FUEL SUPPLY WITH ELECTRICITY DEMAND

In an ideal world, every power project supplies customers who use the same amount of electricity every day of the year. Unfortunately, weather dramatically impacts electricity demand as cold and hot temperatures lead to spikes in heating and cooling. For example, an electricity plant's daily gas consumption in the low season may be half of its daily demand during the high season. When the fuel supplier manages the power project's seasonal swing, it must reserve sufficient production, processing, and pipeline capacity for peak demand, even if these facilities are only utilized on one day. Over the course of a year, this can lead to economic waste from underutilized production, processing, and pipeline capacity.

Other solutions to seasonal swing include

- *Counter-swing customers.* The ideal scenario for managing a power project's seasonal swing is to identify a second fuel customer that can purchase fuel when the power project does not. For example, a Middle Eastern gas supplier might sell gas to Dubai electricity plants in the summer when air-conditioning demand is high and LNG to the Asian market during its cold winter, when heating demand is high.
- *Peaking gas from a second gas source.* A peaking gas arrangement usually involves two GSPAs from two production sources, one with a flat, predictable gas flow and a second that provides the incremental gas that the power project needs during periods of peak demand. For example, the power project may purchase associated gas in the summer from a crude oil field that would otherwise re-inject the gas during the rest of the year.
- *Storage.* It is possible to produce and transport natural gas at a relatively flat rate, and then inject any gas that is not consumed on any given day into a storage facility adjacent to the electricity plant. This enables the power project to meet

its peak obligations under a power purchase agreement by burning fuel from both current and past gas production. For example, the power plant might purchase the same quantity of gas every day. The power project consumes as much as it can and the unconsumed quantities are injected into a depleted gas reservoir, which acts as a storage vessel. These stored quantities are later withdrawn and consumed during the power project's peak period. This involves additional costs, such as injection wells, compression, and reprocessing costs. Gas storage is the primary means for managing the seasonal gas demand of customers in North America.

- *Swing management fee.* In the event no solution is available, the fuel supplier will expect the power project to pay for the dormant capacity that it reserves for the seller. The swing management fee represents the seller's lost revenue stream from reserved but unutilized capacity. These costs are then passed along by the power project as higher costs to the electricity consumers under the power purchase agreement.

- *Other approaches.* In my 2008 *Energy Law Journal* article "The Use of Quantity Terms to Improve Efficiency and Stability in International Gas Sales & Purchase Agreements," I describe more complex solutions to calibrating fuel supply and power purchase agreements, including the use of pipeline line pack to create quantity banks that power plants can draw fuel from to meet the highest demand days.[4]

CONCLUSION

The structuring of international power projects is, in many respects, similar to how energy companies structure pipeline projects. Every power project entails a suite of development agreements that

---

4 Scott Gaille, *The Use of Quantity Terms to Improve Efficiency and Stability in International Gas Sales & Purchase Agreements,* 29 ENERGY LAW JOURNAL 645 (2008).

grant the power consortium the right to build, own, and operate the electricity plant. The more complex commercial issue involves aligning the fuel input of the project with electricity sales. Two agreements, typically a gas sales and purchase agreement (on the input side) and a power purchase agreement (on the output side), must be carefully aligned to protect both the power project consortium and the supplier of fuel.

CHAPTER 12

FINANCING INTERNATIONAL ENERGY PROJECTS

T he financing of energy projects is not the focus of this book, but it is important for international business developers to have a basic understanding of the capital channels used by private and public companies of varying sizes to finance projects. The largest oil and gas companies are able, for the most part, to finance their new projects through earnings from the sale of their existing production. In contrast, smaller companies likely have to raise capital for each new acquisition. This creates a chicken-and-the-egg problem as smaller companies may find it difficult to acquire new projects without evidence of their capability to fund them and investors will be reluctant to commit to funding without a secure project. Further, some investors are willing to offer capital to both private and public companies while others only invest in public entities. All factors being equal, this means that a publicly traded energy company usually has access to more of the global investor pool than a similarly situated private company. Private companies must carefully balance the potential benefits of additional capital against the costs and burden of becoming a public company.

PRIVATE COMPANY FINANCING OPTIONS

Energy companies generally begin as private entities that initially raise capital through individual and company relationships and then advance to financial institutions as the business plan is executed. Private companies access capital through one or more of the following channels:

- *Partnering.* A private company that acquires an international energy project can engage in a variety of partnering activities, including farm outs and joint venture agreements. Pursuant to such an arrangement, the company surrenders some equity in the project to a better-financed company that can carry the smaller company through its financial obligations (by paying the smaller company's share of costs). The greater the amount of future costs, the less project equity the seller is allowed to retain. Whereas a company may sell half of its interest to be carried on an exploration well or two, it may be required to divest up to 90 percent of its equity in a project to be carried through a multibillion-dollar development plan.
- *Asset-backed lending.* Pipelines and power projects may secure project financing based on the cash flows from tariffs or power purchase agreements. In the upstream sector, a company can secure asset-based debt facilities on the basis of cash flows from producing reserves. These facilities generally require periodic interest payments, and the production cash flows will need to be sufficient to meet these obligations. A typical bank's approach is to discount the oil price by 25 percent (e.g., assume $60 oil instead of $80 oil) and then calculate the net present value of cash flows from the proved reserves. The bank will usually lend one-half to two-thirds

of this lower oil price NPV. One issue with revolving debt facilities is that the lending ceiling usually floats along with oil and gas prices. If commodity prices crash, the lending ceiling may fall below the debt balance, which can lead to default. In such a case, the company must immediately pay the difference between what is owed and the new ceiling— or risk foreclosure on the asset.

- *Mezzanine option.* Mezzanine options are typically a hybrid debt vehicle in which petroleum investors have an upside component in the form of an overriding royalty or net profits interest (as equity participation in a project). The equity upside enables such investors to assume additional risk. The interest payments in these transactions may be rolled into the principal balance, which further helps small companies manage their cash flows. Mezzanine financing is ideal for development capital situations in which production is accelerating or during the months or years before cash flow is sufficient to service principal and interest on a traditional debt facility.

- *Volumetric option.* Debt financing can be structured as an advance of funds to be repaid with a specific quantity of future production instead of cash. This is essentially a presale of production in which the borrower assumes the risk of the failure to produce petroleum and the lender assumes the risk of commodity prices.

- *Lines of equity.* Most private companies engaged in large-scale international exploration and production are financed by lines of equity. Several large-cap private equity funds, such as Riverstone, Warburg, and Blackstone, have entered into funding obligations with international petroleum companies. These funds typically acquire a controlling interest in the energy company in exchange for funding all of its financial obligations through capital contributions. The principal advantage of private equity funding is that the management team can demonstrate to asset sellers and governments that the company has the financial capability to acquire and develop opportunities. The primary disadvantage is that the private equity fund provides a limited amount of time for the management team to execute the business plan. After three to five years, the private equity fund will look to sell the company. Sales proceeds are first used to repay the capital provided by the private equity fund. The founding management team can expect to receive approximately 20 percent of the net profits of the sale, with the balance flowing to the private equity fund.

- *Private offerings.* U.S. companies can also offer securities (equity or debt) to sophisticated investors through private placements (e.g., Rule 144A). Private offerings are often an interim step toward a company becoming public.

PUBLIC COMPANY FINANCING OPTIONS

As a company grows, the question of becoming public inevitably arises, usually in the course of trying to raise capital for new projects. Access to additional capital channels is the principal reason a private company becomes public and takes on the additional costs and burden of public company regulation. Public companies have access to all of the private capital channels plus additional public market capital channels:

- *Public offerings.* Public companies can raise capital through the public sale of their common stock. This can take place during an initial public offering of the stock and then repeatedly over time through secondary offerings. Through a series of secondary offerings, a public company can raise capital in steps, over time, as it grows.
- *Private investment in public equity (PIPE).* Public companies are popular with hedge funds, which seek to privately purchase shares at a discount to the market price. These types of placements can be more efficient fund-raising vehicles for smaller companies because they do not require road shows and can be done more quickly than broader public offerings.
- *Stock as acquisition currency.* Publicly traded stock has a market value that better enables it to be used as an alternative

to cash in acquisitions. For example, a seller may assign its asset to a publicly traded company in exchange for shares in the company (instead of cash). Similarly, it is easier for a public company to acquire another company through merger by issuing publicly traded shares in exchange.

- *Bonds, preferred stock, convertible instruments, and warrants.* Public company investors can use a variety of debt and equity capital channels to entice investors to provide capital. Investors typically are more comfortable making such investments with public companies because of the anticipated liquidity of the stock, transparency of financial reporting, and clarity of market values.

PUBLIC ADVANTAGES AND DISADVANTAGES

In addition to the capital raising advantages discussed above, public companies can offer the owner of a private company additional benefits, such as

- *Wealth creation.* The price and earnings multiples that investors receive for private companies are usually in the low single digits, whereas multiples can be ten to twenty times or more for public companies. Illiquidity of private shares, lack of transparency with respect to private company financials, less access to capital, and less scrutiny with respect to regulatory and legal compliance, among other factors, can contribute to shares in a private concern being worth much less than those in a public company.
- *Owners' liquidity.* Management and employees find it easier to sell public shares from time to time to fund their personal financial needs. Private equity can be difficult to sell and there may be prohibitions on partial sales by only some of the private owners. Differing views on when to sell a private company can strain the relationship among its owners. In contrast, shareholders in a public company can sell in part

or whole as they would like, subject to restrictions on insider trading.

- *Estate planning.* In the event of a death, a private company owner may be forced to sell the entire business interest to pay estate taxes, often at a greatly reduced valuation. The market establishes public company share valuations and shares can be readily sold in part, as necessary, to raise funds for estate taxes.
- *Hiring and retention.* A public company's ability to offer stock options, restricted stock, and other such awards facilitates the hiring and retention of the best employees.

In contrast to these benefits, public companies have numerous costs and complications. The cost of becoming a public company can be seven figures in an initial public offering (IPO) and six figures in a reverse merger. Ongoing legal, accounting, and audit costs can also add significantly to overhead.

Public companies are required to disclose considerably more information about their businesses. The disclosure requirements can themselves be burdensome in terms of the amount of time employees spend on compliance. Furthermore, the additional disclosure requirements may signal to competitors where a company's next acquisitions will be and otherwise weaken one's competitive advantage.

Finally, the scrutiny of the public (and shareholder) expectations can be distracting for management. Executives may feel compelled to deliver quarter-over-quarter growth. This can place pressure on the company to make acquisitions too quickly, which can lead to less profitable acquisitions. Such external concerns have the potential to distort management decisions.

The Public Company Compliance Burden

In addition to annual and quarterly filings with the Securities and Exchange Commission (SEC), some aspects of the public company compliance burden in the United States are

- *Form 8-K/Regulation FD.* In between quarterly filings, companies also must publicly disclose material developments through the filing of a press release or Form 8-K.
- *Insider trading.* U.S. securities law describes illegal insider trading as "buying or selling a security, in breach of a fiduciary duty or other relationship of trust and confidence, while in possession of material, nonpublic information about the security." This also includes "'tipping' such information [to third parties], securities trading by the person 'tipped,' and securities trading by those who misappropriate such information." Examples of prohibited insider trading include "Corporate officers, directors, and employees who trade the corporation's securities after learning of significant, confidential corporate developments; friends, business associates, family members, and other 'tippees' of such officers, directors, and employees, who trade the securities after receiving such information; [and] Employees of law, banking, brokerage and printing firms who were given such information to provide services to the corporation whose securities they trade." The law prohibits these types of insider trading because the practice "undermines investor confidence in the fairness" of the markets.
- *Rule 10b5-1 stock trading plans.* One way the SEC allows insiders to avoid the risk of investigations related to insider trading is to enact a stock trading plan that, for example, enables an officer of the company to agree in advance to sell a certain amount of stock periodically and without discretion. Because the decision to sell the stock is made many months in advance of the sale, such plans insulate executives from allegations that the trading decision was made as a consequence of inside information.
- *Insider securities ownership reporting requirements.* Any director, officer, or 10 percent owner of a public company is required to file reports of their transactions in the company's securities. Generally, a company files these forms on behalf of its officers.

- *Short-swing profits.* U.S. law requires directors, officers, and 10 percent owners to disgorge their profits from short-swing sales—that is, a purchase and sale, or a sale and purchase, of securities occurring within a six-month period.
- *Short sales by insiders.* U.S. law prohibits officers, directors, and 10 percent owners from short selling the company's shares.
- *Market manipulation.* Securities laws prohibit market manipulation—transactions that tend to create an artificial price or maintain an artificial price for a stock.
- *Sarbanes–Oxley Act.* The Sarbanes–Oxley Act includes accounting and finance personnel background checks, independent board members serving on the audit committee, certification of the accuracy of financial statements by the CEO and CFO, reporting of securities law violations, prohibition of personal loans by a company to its executive officers, and internal controls and procedures for financial reporting.

REVERSE MERGERS COMPARED TO IPOs

The two principal routes for becoming a public company are an initial public offering (IPO) and a reverse merger. An IPO is the first sale of stock by a private company to the public, which requires various regulatory processes and the assistance of an underwriting firm. In a reverse merger, a private company becomes public indirectly by merging into a company that has already completed the public offering process.

After a reverse merger, the owners of a private company obtain control of the publicly traded company. The public company is typically a "shell" that previously owned assets but no longer does; at some point in the past, its assets were sold. Rather than dissolving a company that invested more than a million dollars in the regulatory process to become public, the owners of the shell make additional expenditures to keep the dormant company on a public market (even though it has no assets). The owners will then look for an opportunity to sell the value of the public company's position to another private company. The reverse merger takes place when the owner of a private company exchanges its ownership in the private company for the vast majority of the public company's shares.

As such, a reverse merger is a way for a private company to accelerate the public process by immediately purchasing the value of the time, legal, regulatory, marketing, and underwriting investment undertaken by another company several years before. This makes it easier to become a public company, but it also means that many companies that opt for this route do so with unrealistic expectations of their capitalization, business plan, and attractiveness to the public market. The IPO process and its underwriters weed out all but the strongest, most attractive companies. In contrast, many companies that have little chance of success on the public market get there through reverse mergers. These organizations may suffer from low valuations and a lack of institutional following while enduring regulatory and legal costs.

Nonetheless, if a company is a strong, growing entity with a good story that the market finds attractive, a reverse merger can be successful. Advantages of a reverse merger include

- *Less dilution.* A reverse merger does not result in the sale of any stock. At the time of the merger, a small percentage (typically in the single digits) of the company's ownership is transferred to the existing public shareholders (and others who coordinate the reverse merger). After that, dilution occurs opportunistically, at the discretion of the initial owners. This enables the initial owners to grow the company in steps over time. As the company expands and its market capitalization increases, the cost (in terms of percentage dilution) decreases with each successive secondary stock offering. For example, if a company's market capitalization is $100 million in Year One, a $10 million capital raise would dilute the company by about 10 percent; if the market capitalization in Year Two is $200 million, a $10 million capital raise would dilute the company by about 5 percent.

In contrast, an IPO might dispose of one-half of the company at the $100 million market capitalization point. This process of staging secondary offerings, particularly for a company with a steep growth trajectory, should lead to less dilution over time.

- *More control.* Less dilution also means that the founders should be able to maintain control over the company for a longer period of time.
- *Available to smaller companies.* Due to costs such as underwriting and materiality thresholds for investment banks, the IPO process is generally only available to large companies.
- *Less expensive.* The reverse merger process typically costs less than the IPO process due to the absence of underwriting costs and somewhat lower legal fees. Much of the cost of a reverse merger is cashless due to the owners of the shell company being compensated by stock in the new enterprise (as opposed to cash).
- *Faster time frame.* If the public company being acquired is already reporting and current with its SEC filings, the reverse merger can be completed within weeks. In contrast, an IPO can take many months, including periods of waiting on comments from regulators.
- *No IPO window.* The reverse merger can be accomplished at any time, irrespective of market conditions. The market for IPOs, often referred to as the IPO window, may close, causing delays. Even if it quickly reopens, additional due diligence and audit costs may be incurred to update documents. If the window closes, the underwriter may abort the IPO, requiring the company to start again with a new underwriter.

Disadvantages of a reverse merger include

- *No capital raised.* The reverse merger itself does not raise any capital. Capital is only raised in subsequent secondary offerings of the company's stock. If an IPO is successful, substantial capital is raised at the time the company becomes public. This provides owners with some assurance that a market exists for their stock.

- *Liquidity problems.* A reverse merger typically results in a stock being traded on the over-the-counter (OTC) market, which has limited liquidity. Shares may be difficult to sell, which defeats some of the advantages of being a public company. Liquidity problems may only be resolved when the company is able to meet the standards for trading on a larger exchange such as the AMEX or NASDAQ.
- *Limited sponsorship.* A reverse merger requires the company to build its own sponsorship over time through the use of investor relations firms and secondary offering underwriters.
- *Low visibility.* Reverse mergers usually start on the OTC market and the company will eventually need to apply to a larger exchange when it can meet the appropriate requirements. IPOs typically trade on only the large, high-visibility stock exchanges.
- *Hidden liabilities.* At the time of a reverse merger, the private company will expose its assets to any liabilities of the public company. It is important that the public company being acquired is clean and free from potential liabilities. Because an IPO does not involve any other company, no such risk exists.

Another way to think about a reverse merger is that it accomplishes the same thing as an IPO, but in two stages. The first stage is the public presence, which is immediately achieved with a reverse merger. After this has occurred, the company engages investor relations firms and secondary underwriters to grow its shareholder base and raise capital. The success of the follow-on stage will depend on the quality of the company's assets, its growth rate, and the successful execution of its business plan. As a general rule, the market rewards success and the company should be able to grow its market capitalization and graduate from the over-the-counter market to a major stock exchange.

CONCLUSION

Energy projects demand significant capital costs that require parallel approaches to fund-raising in conjunction with business development. While funding can often be secured privately through joint ventures, banks, and private placements, these private sources account for only a portion of the international investment community. Much of the world only invests in publicly traded companies, and the ability to access these investors requires a company to become public. Large companies can undertake a traditional IPO, but smaller organizations may access public markets through a reverse merger into an existing public company.

CHAPTER 13

GOVERNMENT DISPUTES

I nternational projects entail political risk. Governments may view energy contracts as flexible and subject to revision as circumstances change over time. A regime change may render suspect those energy companies that had a close relationship with the past ruler. Wars, sanctions, and unresolved international border disputes can delay or prevent the development of energy projects. As hard as a company may work to maintain a good relationship with the host government, disputes can and will arise over multidecade projects.

CHANGED COMMERCIAL CIRCUMSTANCES

It is erroneous for a company to assume that the terms of its initial contracts with a government will survive entirely intact over the duration of a project. As years and decades pass, the reality of actual revenues and costs can diverge greatly from the assumptions on which the project was originally based. Changed circumstances in the favor of the foreign company can lead the government to reopen the commercial terms of the transaction.

Paired with the risk of changed economics is the reality that an energy company's investments in another country are essentially captive. The infrastructure for an upstream development or pipeline can easily cost billions of dollars. Much of it is immoveable. This gives the host government a significant advantage when it comes to renegotiating contracts.

Capital-intensive offshore development

Host governments often find increased revenues from commodity price movements to be particularly objectionable because the contractor's profits rise irrespective of individual performance. For example, what happens if the economic model assumes an oil price of $20 per barrel and oil prices rise to and remain at $100 per barrel? This type of movement can cause the rate of return to skyrocket, leaving the foreign contractor in a position where it makes more than anticipated. In such cases, a company can expect that the government will seek to renegotiate the terms of the agreement on the basis of changed circumstances.

What happens when circumstances change in favor of the government? Officials are usually unreceptive to changing the terms of a contract to reestablish the original economic equilibrium when it has become disadvantageous for the company. The government may view the company as having made a mistake and may believe it fair for the company to suffer because its assumptions were incorrect. Moreover, the negative economic circumstances that lead a company toward renegotiation usually impact the government's revenues, as well. A government that fuels its budget with cash from oil revenues may be staring at budgetary shortfalls from other projects that make relief for the contractor unlikely.

Notwithstanding this double standard and the resistance a company may face from the host government, the company may want to approach the government to open a dialogue. These discussions can be difficult. Firstly, the government will almost always want full disclosure of the project economics. If the impact of changed circumstances on the company is that the project is merely less profitable—for example, a 30 percent rate of return has become a 20 percent rate of return—the government is unlikely to be receptive. However, if the project has become truly uneconomic, to the point where the company may consider leaving the country or shutting down the project, the government will be more amenable.

A company should always remember that any time it reopens the terms and conditions of the contract with the host government, it is likely that the host government will have its own list of changes or issues. A discussion that starts on one metric can quickly expand to include many different provisions or terms. As such, a company should only reopen host government contracts under dire circumstances.

In light of recent commodity prices, production sharing agreements in the upstream sector now routinely contain formulaic provisions that automatically increase the government's share of profit oil as the contractor's rate of return increases. This ensures that changes in economics do not result in outsize gains for the foreign contractor. Companies may also prefer these clauses because they can help to increase the stability and predictability of international contracts and can provide some economic relief if circumstances change in the government's favor (for example, if oil prices fall).

SANCTIONS

International energy projects can sometimes be caught in the crossfire of international disputes between the host government and the company's jurisdiction. Just as a positive political relationship (or the desire to advance one) can strengthen a company's position in a foreign country, so can deterioration of political relationships have fallout for a company. Fortunately, the pace of international relations is slow and the imposition of sanctions rarely comes as a great surprise.

As tensions build between the United States (or European nations) and a government in which a company has an energy project, it may need to consider exit options. One negative aspect of leaving under such circumstances is that the company is effectively a distressed seller, and potential buyers will expect a discount. Further, the number of companies that are potential buyers is likely to be substantially curtailed by the same circumstances that are causing the exit in the first place. If all American companies, and perhaps all European companies, are avoiding investment in a particular country, the number of financially capable buyers will likely be a fraction of the market that might have existed in the absence of increased political risk. A seller will need to weigh the discount in the marketplace, assuming that a potential buyer can even be found, against the risk that the project will be affected by sanctions.

The impact of sanctions can be devastating. One or more governments may immediately forbid all companies under their jurisdiction from engaging in the petroleum business with the host government. Overnight, a company can lose all revenues from a project into which it has sunk billions of dollars. It then faces an uncertain time line of when, if ever, it can return. The company will be forced to evacuate its personnel, and the remaining partners— or the host government's national oil company—will then assume operational responsibility for the project. In order to avoid violations of its agreements, the departing company will issue declarations of force majeure under all of its contracts.

Most international contracts contain force majeure clauses. These provide that any company's failure to perform its obligations is excused if circumstances beyond its reasonable control arise. Sanctions fall into the category of force majeure because a company is told that it is now against the law to do business in the host country. As such, the company has no choice but to comply with the laws of *its* nation, and it would not be fair to subject an organization to claims of damage for nonperformance.

Notwithstanding a declaration of force majeure, the host government may not have sympathy. It may expropriate the project on the basis that the guest company is unable to fulfill its contractual terms. Or it may take the project away as retribution against the government imposing the sanctions. In these cases, the sanctions impose a permanent loss on the company.

Depending on the company's track record in the host country and its relationship with the government, it may be possible to avoid expropriation. A company can sometimes negotiate an arrangement that allows for it to return to its concession in the future if and when sanctions are lifted. These arrangements are usually referred to as suspension agreements. At the highest level, a suspension agreement involves the oil company temporarily granting to the government all of its rights and entitlements to production (or other revenues) in exchange for the government assuming responsibility for the company's obligations, whether in the form of costs or operations responsibility. This is easier to accomplish if the government has a national oil company capable of managing the project. If the government has to look to other companies to step in and operate the field, it may be harder to reach agreement on suspension terms. The replacement company will usually want some assurance of a permanent grant of rights; a temporary right to production may be insufficient consideration. Assuming that the government can practically operate the field, a suspension arrangement avoids uncertainties around the invocation of force majeure clauses—and the arbitrations that can subsequently be brought by companies whose force majeure rights are not respected.

When a suspension arrangement comes to an end, such as when sanctions are lifted, the prior contractual arrangements automatically spring back to life. The guest company is restored to its share of production as well as to its obligation to fund and potentially to operate the field. Transitional periods can be built into the suspension agreement to make this process smoother.

There also is the question of whether one or the other party would like the suspension agreement to be indefinite or limited in duration. Some sanctions have been imposed for decades. During long periods, the petroleum in a field can be depleted, leaving a guest company with little desire to resume ownership. Moreover, it is unlikely that a government suffering under sanctions will reinvest capital into properly maintaining the facilities and wells. This can lead to liabilities for repairs and abandonment costs. A company has to weigh and anticipate the timing of the suspension agreement to avoid the possibility that it will forsake all of the revenue but one day be left with an environmental and abandonment mess and the liabilities that go with it.

Unresolved International Border Disputes

Looking at a map of the world, it would appear that the boundaries of nations are well delineated. The reality is quite a bit different. In Africa alone, there are several dozen international border disputes in which two countries claim the same territory as their own. Sometimes these are land disputes and other times they are maritime-based. The stakes for determining which country owns rights to offshore petroleum resources are very high, and the drawing of maritime boundaries is a complex process that seeks to extend lines from the onshore boundary into the ocean. Fairly small differences in the direction of this line at the starting point on land can result in significant portions of offshore petroleum rights shifting from the jurisdiction of one nation to another.

Such disputed areas are, practically speaking, off-limits to oil and gas exploration during the pendency of dispute. Notwithstanding the inability to undertake work, different oil companies may have licensed the same disputed territory from each of the two governments involved. Should one of the companies seek to acquire seismic data or drill a well in the disputed area, it is likely that the other country will send its military to intervene. Even in the absence of an overt threat, why would a company risk capital to discover petroleum that may end up belonging to someone else?

These questions are rarely confronted because it is usually the case that neither of the countries involved in the dispute will ultimately approve any petroleum operations in a disputed area. After all, if operations are successful, it will merely make a resolution of the border dispute (and compromise) more difficult. Moreover, the nations are likely to prohibit petroleum exploration not only in the disputed area but in any nearby areas, as well. A discovery of oil *near* a disputed area can similarly increase the contentious nature of the border resolution process and prolong it further.

In an ideal world, different views on the location of international borders can be settled through compromise. This includes splitting the difference between the perpendicular lines and allowing each nation to take roughly half of the disputed section. The disputed area may be placed in a joint development zone in which all petroleum production in the disputed area is shared between the two countries. There are several joint development zones along the oily West African coast.

The joint development zone approach can be attractive to both countries because it avoids the risk that an oilfield in the disputed zone happens to reside on the wrong side of the line, leaving one country with nothing. The petroleum company, though, is generally indifferent to whether a petroleum block lies within a country or a joint development zone, assuming similar fiscal terms. The government taxes that would have otherwise gone to just one nation are shared among two.

One of my prior companies saw an attractive exploration prospect in one of these disputed zones. Neither country had licensed the exploration acreage in the area of dispute. We approached both nations in parallel, seeking to license the disputed area. Our approach was to pay bonuses to each of the governments to secure the acreage and then have the governments simultaneously agree to place the obligation to conduct any work in suspension, pending resolution of the border. In this way, our company sought to acquire a future option on the prospect—no matter how the border dispute was resolved. While we ultimately succeeded in obtaining the licenses, our approach created considerable political problems. Both nations objected to the fact that we were seeking to do business with its "enemy." The general view of both governments was that the very act of a company licensing the acreage twice somehow undermined each country's certain view that its maritime claims were undeniable.

Political issues can practically force a company to choose sides in an international border dispute. This can sometimes be facilitated by the location of prospects. If a greater portion of a prospect sits closer to Country A, then that is the horse to bet on. An approach that I have used in the past is to license the acreage in the location where the prospects are closest to the undisputed waters and then enter into a suspension agreement. The suspension agreement preserves the rights of the company, effectively freezing its obligation to undertake exploration. This circumstance limits the amount of dollars that are placed at risk by the company because typically the only expenditure is a signature bonus. Nonetheless, the company must be prepared for a long wait, of perhaps decades, before a definitive resolution of the border can occur. A small company and its investors would probably not have the financial staying power to pay a signature bonus that may not have a return associated with it for many, many years.

REGIME CHANGE

The developing world has a long record of regime changes. Today's forever is tomorrow's forgotten. Companies rightly worry that a contract duly negotiated with one regime may not be respected by its inevitable successor. Nonetheless, petroleum companies and their contracts usually survive regime changes relatively intact. In part, this is because the regime, be it old or new, needs the company to assist it in developing and producing its natural resources. The cash flow from the sale of petroleum is as essential to the man who took office yesterday as it was to the one who ruled for thirty years. In most cases, these nations' national oil companies do not have the same financial resources or technical capability as international oil companies. Even if this is not the case, the new leadership may want to court favor with the home nation of the IOCs. Be it the United States or the European Union, the expropriation of their companies' assets is unlikely to get the new regime off on favorable political footing. Such practical concerns generally contribute to the survivability of contracts (and companies) from one regime to the next.

The exceptions to this rule generally arise when the new regime puts political ideology above pragmatism. South America has been a particularly troublesome area for international oil companies in recent decades due to the anti-Americanism and socialist tendencies of regional political leaders. In cases where the new regime is overtly hostile to a guest company's home nation, survivability becomes more challenging. To the extent that a new regime has entered office under the mantra of retaking national resources, the practical question of whether or not the state oil company can efficiently develop the resources may become secondary to politics.

In contrast to South America, Sub-Saharan African regime change tends to be more about power and less about ideology. The result for international oil companies is that the group of people running the country may change, but in the absence of other problems, contracts tend to remain intact and business goes on as usual. The new leaders wish to have access to petroleum cash flows and usually will not take any steps that would place income at risk. However, if a company is viewed as too cozy with the prior regime or if charges of corruption are leveled at the prior rulers' award of energy concessions, particular companies' rights could be at risk.

The moment a regime change takes place, it is important for a company to send a high-level representative to meet with the new oil minister and other officials. The presentation should start with an overview of the company's projects in the country and an explanation of how the relationship between the company and the country adds value to the development of its resources. Presenting the new oil minister with such knowledge will help him or her understand your value and be better able to explain your company to the new leader. The executive can also offer to educate the minister about other projects or the nation's energy resources more generally. Relationships and impressions are often forged in the early days of an official taking office. When a company sends a senior executive to meet with the new oil minister, it conveys the message that the company is enthusiastic about working with the new government and will be a helpful, cooperative partner.

VIOLENCE

Force majeure can include not only disagreements with governments, but also the inability of a government to control events within its borders. There can be small or large exchanges of violence with neighboring nations. More commonly, developing world nations may be unable to maintain basic law and order over its own citizens. Petroleum companies need to be aware of the types of risks for violence that exist in different nations and in parts of those nations, and take steps to mitigate them and protect its personnel.

Just because a geographic area is within the recognized international borders of a nation does not mean that all, or some portion, of the people who live there acknowledge or respect the rule of the government. In Angola, for example, one of its states is the oil-rich enclave of Cabinda. Cabinda is not geographically connected to the rest of Angola proper, and the land route to Cabinda province requires transit through a swath of the Democratic Republic of Congo. Cabinda had formerly been the Portuguese Congo, but through a treaty in the 1970s, the Portuguese government transferred the governance of Cabinda to Angola. The Cabindans did not approve the treaty and maintain that they are culturally and ethnically distinct from Angolans. Some Cabindans wage political and military movements for independence. Periodic attacks by the rebels make onshore oil and gas activities in Cabinda potentially dangerous and subject to prolonged periods of force majeure.

Author standing next to damaged armored vehicle in Angola

Kidnapping can also be a problem for international energy development. Kidnappings may take place for political or economic reasons, or both. I spent a considerable amount of time doing business in Colombia at a time when kidnappings for ransom were an occasional problem. Executives in Colombia often traveled in motorcades with "chase" cars containing armed guards to discourage kidnapping attempts. Even lower-level employees typically had a driver and security escort. This was not necessarily enough, though. An employee stepped off a Continental Airlines flight with his spouse and was met by a company driver and security guard. En route to their hotel, the guard and driver were overpowered by assailants who kidnapped the employee and his wife. Eventually, the two were released with minor injuries. Such events can make it difficult for a company to recruit and maintain quality personnel.

Other regions face the threat of gangs who target Western travelers or residents for smash-and-grab robberies. In Lagos, Nigeria, an American executive was riding in the backseat of a car on his way from the airport to his hotel when truckloads of armed men overtook the vehicle on the airport road. His guards fled, leaving him at the mercy of the attackers. They took all of his luggage, his belongings, and his passport and made him strip completely naked on the side of the road. When he could not take off his wedding ring fast enough, one of the assailants retrieved a pair of rose clippers and proceeded to prepare for the removal of the man's finger. Fortunately, the ring came off on its own accord. The executive was left naked on the side of the road and had to walk several miles back to the airport, sustaining cuts from broken glass along the way. Many vehicles and taxis passed him without stopping to offer assistance. Only after he reached the airport did security officials contact the U.S. Embassy, from which officials came to retrieve him.

Natural Disasters

Natural disasters can threaten international projects, as well. Earthquakes, floods, volcanoes, typhoons and other acts of God can damage facilities and otherwise disrupt a project. Force majeure clauses typically operate to protect projects and their operators from any liability caused by such circumstances, but the loss of revenues will still harm the company. As such, it is important to consider to what extent a project portfolio is exposed to different kinds of natural risks and to understand what precautions have been taken in anticipation and what contingency plans exist. Proper preparation for natural calamities also can minimize friction with the government, as officials will be looking to energy revenues to help the country's recovery efforts. Whereas companies in developed nations may be able to rely on the government to quickly restore infrastructure following a disaster, the timeline to recovery in a developing nation can be much longer. The company's disaster recovery plan should assume that it will have to independently restore any required infrastructure.

Volcano erupting near Goma, Democratic Republic of Congo

CONCLUSION

Political risk is an inherent part of international energy development. Contracts may be viewed as flexible understandings in the developing world, which can result in host governments seeking to renegotiate contractual terms based on perceptions of changed circumstances. Sanctions can be imposed, effectively denying a company the right to do business in certain parts of the world and placing its assets there at risk. Unresolved international borders can delay for decades a development near a disputed boundary. Relationships with host governments can be strained by regime change or the inability of the government to protect a company's operations and personnel from violence. Any of these events can lead to disputes, declarations of force majeure, or mutually agreed upon suspensions of performance.

CHAPTER 14

DISPUTE RESOLUTION

W hen a dispute between companies of the same nationality escalates to the point where the parties can no longer resolve it, recourse to the judicial process is the usual remedy and the victorious party can enforce the judgment. This is not generally the case with international energy development. Enforcement of contracts across borders is more difficult, and even if one party to the dispute obtains a judgment, the ability to collect on the award is questionable. If the dispute involves a host government, a company must add to its concerns the repercussions of filing any claim at all. Will the host government expropriate the company's assets in retaliation? Will the company ever be awarded another project in the country?

HOST GOVERNMENT DISPUTES

As discussed in the previous chapter, there are many ways that a host government and guest company can become embroiled in conflict. Circumstances change, particularly over contractual periods lasting twenty, thirty, or more years. It may be the case that a government makes a request that goes too far or no compromise or trade is possible. In such circumstances, the foreign company should be prepared to have the change forced upon it.

The company's first response should be to express its disagreement respectfully. It should use the usual means of communication and persuasion to try to prevent or soften the action but should avoid threatening arbitration. If adverse actions do come, the company should coolly analyze the situation. While it may feel unfairly treated by a host government, the economic results may not be as bad as expected.

Senior executives should not underestimate the distorting effects of emotion on the company's initial reaction after a foreign government has ignored or violated its contract. Of particular concern is the response of the in-country general manager, who may take the government's action personally. The general manager should play only a peripheral role in resolving such disputes.

The rest of the company's team should independently examine the economic impact and ask questions such as

- If the project were being offered on the new terms, would it be an acceptable investment?
- If the company has other investments in the country, how does the change influence the overall economics of the countrywide investments? The overall impact may be very small.

The point is that a company must avoid overreacting. Any company has three choices to consider: (1) live with the decision; (2) divest; or (3) arbitrate.

- *Option 1: Live with it.* Unless economic value is completely destroyed, the best course of action is to accept the change. Some considerations weighing in the direction of acceptance include:
  - ➢ *Future business in the country*. The smaller the country, the longer is its memory. If there is any chance that your

company will want to do business in the host country at some point in the future, it is a good reason to grin and bear it.

➢ *Regional or international reputation.* Do not underestimate how a bad relationship in one country can make it harder to do business elsewhere. Arbitration, even if you win, can make other governments leery of doing business with you, and divestment can make them question your long-term commitment.

➢ *Replacement cost.* While difficult to capture on an economic model, having a project and a position in a country has value. Occupying real estate may open other opportunities. It costs the company money and human capital to capture any position. It could take years to build a similar position in another region.

➢ *Your turn may come.* It may be possible to improve your company's situation in the future simply because the individuals in the government change. You also may be able to use the historical injuries to your company's contractual rights as leverage in future negotiations, even if only through subtle arguments of fairness.

➢ *Other business.* While it may be politically difficult for the host government to comply with a contractual obligation, there may be other avenues for compensating the company. For example, there may be other projects in the country that could be awarded to the company. It is always worth meeting with government officials to discuss how acquiescence on one issue might be rewarded elsewhere. Such thinking may turn an imminent loss into a gain. For example, the state oil company of a West African nation wanted to operate one of my companies' blocks and wanted to acquire a small part of our participating interest but was unwilling to pay cash for it. I agreed to assign the operatorship and some of the working interest in exchange for a nice block interest elsewhere at some point in the future.

About a year later, the government gave my company two block interests as its reward.

- *Option 2: Divest.* Even if your company does not see value in a project, another organization may have a different perspective. This could be because the other company is not subject to U.S. taxation or has broader goals in the host country, such as building a larger presence and an economy of scale. Some advantages to divestment include
  - ➢ *Sales price.* Depending on the circumstances, your company may be able to recoup a large portion of its loss by finding the right buyer. Your company might also consider swapping assets if the buyer has something more attractive elsewhere in the world.
  - ➢ *Future business in the country.* If done properly, divestment should leave the door open for future re-entry. You might express your company's interest at looking at future projects. If you sell to a non-U.S. organization, you can even say that it was the American tax impact that rendered this particular project unattractive under the changed contractual terms. It then becomes a project better suited for a different company. The word *different* is always a good one to use.
  - ➢ *Regional or international reputation.* Coming and going too quickly in too many countries can make governments doubt your staying power, but companies are always buying and selling assets and yours should be able to explain the occasional exit if asked.
- *Option 3: Arbitration.* When I was a young lawyer, an old arbitration specialist once told me, "Only arbitrate if your company is prepared to leave the country forever and never do any business whatsoever there again." Arbitration against a host government should be the last resort. It should only be undertaken when a company's relationship with a country has been substantially destroyed. I was witness to a matter involving a tax dispute on a multibillion-dollar oilfield in South America.

The government increased taxes on the oilfield in violation of the contracts with the company, which ended up costing the company close to $100 million. The company filed for arbitration and prevailed, but the government promptly expropriated the multibillion-dollar asset after losing. The company was left in far worse shape than it would have been had it simply paid the higher taxes. Considerations weighing in favor of arbitration include

➢ *Expropriation.* A government has either entirely expropriated your company's assets or the change is so extreme that their economic value to your company has been substantially destroyed. In such cases, your company is essentially being thrown out of the country anyway and all you are left with is a claim asking for just compensation. When the economic impact is smaller, though, a company should be very reluctant to file a claim because winning may result in retaliation.

➢ *Future opportunities are unlikely.* What are the chances that your company will want to undertake a project in the host country again? Does the country represent a small percentage of the world market share in project opportunities? For example, arbitrating against Angola or Nigeria or some other top petroleum producing country would be expensive in the form of lost future opportunities because there are, and will be, many other technically attractive projects there in the future. A smaller country with fewer prospects would not be as costly.

➢ *High chance of success.* How strong is your company's legal case? Has your company broken any rules in the host country that could support counterclaims? If the government is truly the only bad actor in the dispute, arbitration may have a high probability of success. The problem is that most companies are far from perfect and the government may have its own list of grievances, small or large, that come to the forefront after arbitration is filed. A good rule of thumb is that the strongest case has a two-in-three chance of success and the weakest one has a one-in-three chance. Victory should never be assumed.

➤ *Collection of judgment possible.* Unfortunately, even if a company wins its arbitration, the prospect for collecting on the award may be slim. The host government of a developing nation generally will not (and may not even be able to) pay an arbitral judgment. Even if the government produces oil, its share of oil is usually either consumed domestically or sold to third parties within its own territorial waters. One of the key enforcement factors is whether the government owns assets outside of its borders. For example, does the host government operate an airline that flies to major international airports in nations where an arbitral judgment would be recognized and enforceable? A small oil company obtained a $50-million award against an African nation with a national airline that flew a daily flight to Paris. The company took its judgment to Charles de Gaulle Airport and seized the country's airplane in satisfaction. Within a few hours, $50 million was wired to the company's account and the return flight suffered only a minor delay.

ARBITRATION CONSIDERATIONS

International contracts typically include arbitration clauses. Such clauses are in place to avoid recourse to any particular country's judicial system. To the extent that a government is a party to a contract, it would not be fair for disputes to be resolved in the courts of the host country, assuming that the host country has a developed judiciary system capable of handling complex commercial disputes. Similarly, a jury of Texans might be biased in favor of a local Houston company, thereby denying the host government a fair trial.

The importance of international arbitration extends to international contracts made between two American companies where the subject matter of the contract may be an energy project in another nation. Some courts are reluctant to grant jurisdiction to claims involving property that lies in another nation. The law of jurisdiction can be complex, and it is better to operate under an arbitration clause than risk the possibility of a local court ruling that it has no jurisdiction to hear a breach of contract claim.

Arbitration in a neutral forum, typically with neutral laws, is fairer to both parties and ensures that there is a forum where disputes can be heard. English law is the most common law for international contracts, although host governments often insist that its own law govern the contract. Fortunately, the laws of developing nations on contractual interpretation do not usually differ substantially from English law. In terms of locations, London, Paris, and Geneva tend to be typical venues for arbitrations. This is in part due to the ease of finding qualified arbitrators in those cities.

A single arbitrator or a panel of three arbitrators may hear arbitrations. The panel approach is more typical in high-value contracts, in which case each party appoints one arbitrator (who is in some respects an advocate for its position) and the two party-appointed arbitrators appoint a third chairman of the panel who is ultimately the decision-maker. Single arbitrators appointed by a neutral authority, such as the International Chamber of Commerce (ICC), can decrease the cost of arbitration. While a judicial court's costs are funded mostly by tax dollars, the involved parties fund private arbitration costs through significant administration fees. To the extent that a company may be concerned about smaller claims, it should try to negotiate an arbitration clause that provides for an individual arbitrator.

Parties can save on arbitration costs by providing for ad hoc arbitration as opposed to administered arbitration. Administered arbitration through the International Chamber of Commerce, the London Court of International Arbitration (LCIA), or the American Arbitration Association is more expensive, but if procedural problems arise between the parties, these institutions can step in and resolve them. In an ad hoc arbitration, parties may be forced to resort to courts to resolve procedural issues. Parties must also select a set of rules to govern the arbitration. Administered arbitrations are usually governed by the forum's own rules, such as the Rules of Arbitration of the ICC or the LCIA Arbitration Rules. Ad hoc arbitrations are typically subject to United Nations Commission on Trading Law (UNCITRAL) arbitration rules.

Arbitration awards can be difficult to enforce. The United Nations Convention on the Recognition and Enforcement of Foreign Arbitral Awards (often referred to as the New York Convention) requires the judiciaries of member nations to give effect to arbitration clauses and enforce arbitration awards. As mentioned, a host government on the losing end of a dispute is unlikely to recognize an award, whether or not it is a signatory. Even in disputes between two private companies in different countries, the collection process likely requires significant expenditures on local counsel and the navigation of foreign courts.

CONCLUSION

A company should be cautious about initiating legal action against a host government. A careful examination of the true cost of the government action is required, as well as consideration of the possibility that the project could be sold, before an arbitration is filed. Arbitration against a government should be viewed as a likely end to your company's business relationship with that government. The company should be willing and prepared to lose all of its existing projects in the host country as well as the opportunity for any new projects for years to come. Whether arbitration is lodged against a host government or another company, the enforcement of awards and collection of damages can be difficult.

CHAPTER 15

PROJECT EXITS

O nce involved in a country or project, it can be difficult for a company to divest, or exit. The host government may be able to dictate whether (and to whom) an interest in an existing project can be transferred. The government may examine the creditworthiness or technical capability of the buyer and generally consider whether it prefers the current company or the proposed buyer. The government may also have its own ideas about which company should purchase the project, and the other company may not be willing to pay as much. Such issues can make international divestments a prolonged process.

COORDINATING WITH THE HOST GOVERNMENT

In many international locations, the success (or failure) of a proposed sale depends upon coordinating the process with the host government. This is because most transfers of energy assets require some form of government approval. As such, the host government wants to be the first to know that your company is considering the sale of an asset. Should the oil minister first learn about a company's planned divestment from the press or hear about it from competitors, the government is likely to be offended and will be less cooperative.

By starting the sales process with the government, it may be possible to learn about potential buyers. Companies interested in making investments in the host country are likely to have been in contact with the oil minister. He or she may have made promises to another company that it would be next in line for an investment opportunity.

Even if your company has its own short list of preferred buyers, it is important to prescreen this list with the host government. The oil minister may be able to provide preliminary impressions of potential buyers, indicating companies that it would approve or reject. After all, your company may not be aware of current or prior disputes that may have taken place between certain companies and any given host government. By prescreening buyers, your company can avoid wasting resources on a possible transaction that is unlikely to be approved.

Semantics also can be important when describing a sales process to the host government. Always talk in terms of any sale being "under consideration" and "pending the government's approval." This is true even if you have an agreement of some kind with a third party before you approach the government.

IDENTIFYING THE MARKET

In the absence of any clear guidance from the government regarding specific companies that may be interested in the acquisition, a seller should compose a target list of possible buyers. The problem with international assets is that the list of possible buyers may be very short. The starting point should be other companies already doing business in the nation of divestment. The more international companies participating in a country's energy sector, the greater the likelihood that one of those companies will be a buyer for the asset. In other words, owning assets in countries where there are many international oil companies in competition with one another makes the asset more liquid and easier to sell.

Other factors to consider when evaluating the potential ease of sale include

- *Risk no one else wants.* Many international projects have complex risk profiles, including regime stability; safety of employees due to kidnapping, crime, or terrorism; or potential for force majeure interruptions due to international conflict. At any given time, such events in a country can render even an economically attractive asset illiquid. Similarly, the less risk a country or project has, the greater is the pool of potential buyers.

- *Obligations no one else wants.* Early-life and late-life projects are often difficult to sell because these are times when spending obligations loom large. Commitments to drill many exploration wells or the uncertainty of development costs may encumber early projects. Later-life projects can be similarly burdened by decommissioning costs and environmental concerns.

- *Government interference.* To the extent the host government has a reputation for being difficult, potential buyers may be discouraged from spending a lot of time on due diligence and negotiations out of fear that a transaction may not be approved.

- *Prestige of the seller.* If the seller has an excellent international reputation, the host government may be reluctant to let it sell. Countries often tout the presence of global superstars as investors in their economies. It reflects on the country's ability to be a good partner to business—and on the economic prospects of the nation. Trading away an instantly recognizable corporate name for a smaller company that no one in the country has heard of can be difficult. As such, a seller should focus on companies that the host government will view as comparable (or better).

- *Financial capability.* Large, financially stable companies may be more desirable guests than smaller, financially challenged companies, and a seller should not spend much time marketing an asset to companies that are clearly in a less capable financial position.

- *Good relationship with government.* If the seller has been a great partner and successful operator, ironically, it may have a more difficult time. The devil the government knows may be preferable to the one it does not, and it may be painful for a government bureaucracy to get comfortable with another company's culture and operating approach. In short, "breaking up" with a long-term government partner can be difficult.

- *Bad relationship with government.* More problematic is the situation where a company has somehow offended the host government. A multibillion-dollar transaction in West Africa was not approved by the host government despite the buyer being one of the largest oil companies in the world. While there were several contributing factors to the rejection of the transaction, one appears to have been an executive's use of profanity with the oil minister.

- *Operator versus nonoperator.* Whether or not a company is the operator of a project can impact liquidity. Some potential buyers insist on operating while others want nothing to do with it. Also, the degree to which the government will be involved in a sale increases exponentially if your company is the project operator. This is because nonoperators are viewed as investors—guests who tend to come and go. A government inquiry into the sale of a nonoperating interest usually focuses solely on whether the new company has similar creditworthiness— i.e., is able to pay the bills. Operators typically find the sales process more difficult because they are evaluated on technical capability, as well.

What Happens If the Government Refuses to Approve a Transaction?

Contracts for the sale of international energy interests contain conditions precedent to the closing of the transaction that require the government's approval. This approval must be granted within a certain period of time. If the approval is not received within, for example, six months or one year, then the transaction is automatically terminated.

Keep in mind that the host government may never expressly reject a transaction. It may simply do nothing. By remaining silent, the practical result is usually rejection. Even if the contract with the government deems approval after so many days of silence, the potential buyer will be unlikely to close on a transaction for which the government has not provided its affirmative consent.

Silence can be a form of rejection, but it can also reflect failures in the political process. I was involved in a transaction in Africa where the government's regulation of the petroleum sector was in transition. New laws had been passed that created a new regulatory regime and required all companies with existing rights in oil and gas concessions to convert their old rights into new forms of agreement. The conversion process dragged on for years, as regulators argued over what terms were consistent or inconsistent with the new law. Even though the oil minister had no particular objection to my transaction, no approvals could be granted until the existing concessions were converted into new ones. It is precisely because of circumstances like these that sale and purchase agreements contain long-stop provisions that unwind the transaction if six months or a year pass without the government's approval.

One alternative employed from time to time to address this kind of situation is loosely referred to as a trust arrangement. In this type of transaction, two companies enter into an agreement outside of the government approval process in which the seller (the company with good title in the country) manages the relationship with the government and operates the concession while the buyer (the company without title recognition) enjoys all the economic rights and obligations associated with the property and simply pays the seller to manage and operate it. In effect, the buyer becomes an indirect investor.

The trust arrangement is most common in situations where an existing operator wishes to divest only *part* of its interest in a project and government approval is either not obtained or political circumstances impede the approval. This type of trust arrangement is easier because the seller is already planning to remain in the country as the operator and co-owner of the project. The buyer is merely taking a participation in the project. Nothing changes other than who pays part of the bills and who receives part of the revenues.

Trust arrangements can be advantageous in situations where a company needs to close a transaction quickly. Even if the seller believes that government approval will be obtained, the process of garnering approval can run as long as a year. The economic circumstances of the company or its need for cash to prosecute the work program in the project may require an immediate closing.

Another case when immediate closing may be required is when a well is about to be drilled. The buyer will not want to risk the possibility that the well is successful, thereby creating an incentive for the seller to discourage the government from granting its approval. Waiting a year may simply not be possible. A trust situation can provide a seller with the economic benefits of the transaction immediately and avoid the wait and uncertainty of government approval.

How a trust arrangement is structured is usually dependent on how much of an interest the buyer is acquiring. For example, if the seller owns a 30 percent interest in a project and is selling a 10 percent interest, this transaction is probably best effected through a sale of shares in the offshore company that happens to own the project. Most international project interests are held in special purpose offshore companies in jurisdictions like the Cayman Islands, the British Virgin Islands, Nevis, or Bermuda. Such companies are single asset companies that own only the project interest. As long as the trust arrangement is for less than half of the seller's interest, the easiest way to complete this transaction is by divesting shares. Company documents can then be amended to compel the minority shareholder to pay its pro rata share of the costs and receive its pro rata share of the profits.

Such share divestments generally do not work when the selling company is parting with 50 percent or more of its interest. This is likely to trigger a change-of-control event under the contracts with the host government. In these circumstances, the usual structure is a financing agreement, which is a contractual arrangement (secured by the interest in the underlying asset and likely guaranteed by the parent companies of the buyer and seller) pursuant to which the buyer is contractually required to fund certain costs. In turn, it receives proportionate revenues.

The troubling question is how the host government may react to a trust arrangement, whatever its structure may be. The government may view a trust or partial sale of shares as a circumvention of its approval right. There have been circumstances where similar transactions have been cited as legal grounds by the government for expropriation.

The likelihood that the host government will view a trust arrangement as a bypass of its approval process increases if the government's approval was sought and not obtained. As such, if a seller needs to undertake a transaction and believes there is a chance that government approval will not be forthcoming, the best approach may be to not seek it. If the government were to object at a later date to the transaction, the company can explain that it was a financing transaction and that it had no intention of selling its interest.

The fact of the matter is that these types of transactions rarely stay private forever. For example, if the buyer is a public company, or later becomes a public company, it may be required by securities law to disclose the transaction in its public filings. A company must always weigh the advantages and disadvantages of disclosure to the government and consider how the transaction is described. Many contracts with governments expressly provide for companies to engage in financing transactions in respect of their interest. The best course of action is usually not to seek government approval but to provide a simple courtesy notice letting the government know that the company has engaged in a private financing transaction in respect of the block. By doing so, the company avoids a future surprise or, worse, the allegation of deceit.

Rights of First Refusal or First Offer

In addition to approval rights, the government (and possibly other international companies involved in the project) may hold rights of first offer or refusal. Rights of first offer require a seller to first offer the interest to the government at a certain price. If the government does not accept the price, the seller is free to divest to a third party within a period of several months at a price equal to or greater than the offered price. Rights of first refusal require the seller to first enter into a transaction with a third party. The government then has the right to take the transaction on the same terms and conditions and effectively become the buyer of the interest. From a seller's perspective, rights of first offer are somewhat easier to manage in a sales process because a potential buyer does not have to be concerned with making significant expenditures for due diligence and negotiation only to have someone else take the transaction from it at the last moment.

Governments in the developing world are known to use such rights to their advantage in ways that go beyond the contractual language. Together with approval rights, governments can use rights of first refusal to dictate which company will be the buyer of a property. It is not uncommon for governments to have potential buyers waiting in the wings for an asset divestment. When a sale is announced, the government may state privately that it intends to use its approval or preemptive rights to acquire the asset. Unbeknownst to the seller, the government may be simultaneously negotiating a sale of the same asset to another company.

A government's rationale for back-to-back transactions varies. It may have strategic reasons for delivering the asset to a particular company that may or may not extend beyond the energy sector. For example, the new owner of the asset could be a foreign national oil company from a country such as China. This nation and company may be offering the government loans or economic assistance in addition to the purchase price. It may also be the case that the government's motive is capturing a transaction tax or step-up between the purchase price paid to the selling company and the price it can get for the asset from another company.

In either of these transactions, the selling company may not be able to vend to whomever it wants, nor is it likely that the seller will achieve a sale at market value. The government will likely seek to drive down the sales price as far as possible so that it can create a spread between its acquisition cost and the market value of the secondary sale. Moreover, even if the government is transparent on the sales price, there may be nonprice considerations such as foreign assistance or loan programs. Such considerations may have the practical result of forcing the sale at a discount. If this occurs, the prospective seller may prefer to cancel the sales process and retain the asset.

OVERVIEW OF THE APPROVAL PROCESS

The government approval process varies from country to country. At a minimum, the written approval of the oil or energy minister is required. Other approval requirements may include the state oil company, Parliament, or even the head of state. Informal approvals are also common in the developing world. Do not assume that the process stated in the agreements and the laws of the country is the only one. There may be a complex informal approval process that underlies or precedes the formal approvals. For example, the oil minister may not be allowed to grant an approval before a presidential advisor on energy has signed off on the transaction. Representatives from both companies may need to meet privately with this advisor and the head of state before an approval can be obtained.

The best way to learn about how the process works in practice is to obtain guidance from a local counsel who has been through the approval process with other clients in the past. In most countries, one or two local lawyers represent international energy companies in their dealings with the government. These lawyers have successfully guided other companies and can talk candidly about the twists, turns, and pitfalls.

The provision of credit guarantees may also be part of the process. Energy projects often entail capital obligations in the billions of dollars. Depending on the status of the project, and particularly during exploration and development stage projects, the host government will seek guarantees of financial performance. Large companies typically accomplish this through a limited parent company guarantee. Assuming that the buyer is a shell subsidiary with no other assets, the government will require that a holding company that owns other producing assets provide it with a parent company guarantee. This process may require the company to provide audited financial statements of the guaranteeing entity.

There can be considerable disagreement about the amount of the guarantee. With respect to exploration expenditures, such guarantees typically do not exceed the company's share of minimum exploration expenditures for the current exploration period. In development cases, companies may provide limited guarantees subject to a hard cap denominated in dollars. The exact amount will be a fraction of the development cost expenditures because by this point, performance has been secured, at least in part, by reserves.

An alternative to parent company guarantees is a letter of credit. If there are concerns about the parent company's creditworthiness, the government may require a letter of credit or bank guarantee. In exploration periods, the bank guarantee is usually set at an amount equal to the company's share of its current minimum work program obligations. Bank guarantees are subject to additional costs and typically require the providing company to place in certificates of deposit an amount of cash equal to the guarantee. Because such arrangements can constrain the financial flexibility of the company, most prefer parent company guarantees.

Beyond the ministerial approvals, there are many other bureaucratic hurdles associated with a country exit. If the seller employed local nationals who are not being assumed by the buyer, such persons will receive severance packages under local labor laws. Permits and licenses that were previously obtained will need to be transferred or canceled. These details can take several weeks to months to address.

DISMANTLEMENT, REMOVAL, AND REMEDIATION

International energy projects do not go on forever. At some point, the economic life of the facilities ends. In the case of an oil field, wells need to be plugged and abandoned, surface facilities removed, and environmental damage addressed. At some point, pipelines may be decommissioned. Who pays for these costs when the underlying project is no longer generating revenue?

Many older international project agreements are silent with respect to what happens when the project is over. If the project outlives the rights of the foreign company, the usual outcome is that the government assumes ownership and control. In fact, many pipeline and power development agreements specifically provide for the build-own-operate-transfer model, which allows the foreign company to recoup its investment and return over a period of perhaps twenty or thirty years, with the assets reverting to the government in their entirety. In such cases, does the government have clear responsibility for the abandonment? Or can it or its citizens seek to reach back to the foreign company for liability if there is a mess when the project ends?

To address the risk of litigation years after a company has departed a country, more and more agreements are providing for decommissioning trust funds. Such funds place a portion of the project revenues each year in trust for later cleanup operations. The principal issues surrounding these funds are control and what happens when the fund is too large or too small.

- *Control.* Does the host government, the company, or a third-party financial institution have custody over the DR&R fund?

The government usually argues for receipt of the funds and may be glad to assume responsibility for later cleanup. This leaves the international energy company in a similar position as where the project simply reverts to the government. The government may receive a payment for DR&R each year, but what happens if it uses these payments for general revenue purposes or if the funds otherwise disappear before the DR&R costs are incurred? The company may have a stronger position against claims, but its reputation will still be harmed if there are citizen suits or environmental issues involving one of its former projects. Alternatively, the company can assume liability for the DR&R and receive the funds as additional revenue, which it keeps as a cash reserve on its books. The government may worry in such cases that the company will go bankrupt, have financial issues, or otherwise lose the funds. In light of such concerns, the third-party custodian approach may be the best way to ensure that some funds will be available for DR&R at the project's end.

- *Too little or too much.* Determining the amount of funding needed to decommission a project is not a precise science. Predicting what it will cost to remove and remediate a project thirty years in the future is difficult. Technology could decrease costs. Public perceptions about the extent to which the environment should be restored after a project ends could increase costs. Even if costs are as projected, other circumstances can affect whether the trust fund contains enough money to cover them, including the rate of return achieved in the financial markets over those thirty years, inflation, and how long the project lasts. A project that was expected to produce for thirty years could end in fifteen or it could produce for one hundred years. In the first instance, the fund is likely to be short of money. In the latter case, the accumulation of DR&R funds and their earnings may result in a windfall. Even if the funds are being held in a third-party trust, does the government receive a windfall, or the company? Do they share the windfall? If so, how is it divided? In the case of a DR&R shortfall, is the company responsible for the difference?

CONCLUSION

International project exits are often complicated by the involvement of the host government. Government approval processes may be opaque or prolonged and there is no guarantee that a commercially reasonable transaction will ever be approved. As such, companies investing in international projects should always be mindful of the risk that their ability to divest the project may be limited. In the event that the exit process becomes an issue for a selling company, there are ways to skirt around the approval requirement. Trust arrangements may involve financing agreements through which another company assumes the financial risks and rewards for the project or the sale of a minority stock position in an offshore company. Such structures can enable a company to achieve liquidity from a third party on a faster time line than waiting for a government approval.

CONCLUSION

The last step of the Gaille Method is portfolio construction, which seeks to diversify positions across projects to minimize forms of concentration risk. The best energy project may fall victim to decades of war. Perfect seismic lines may prove dry after a $100-million well expenditure. The most reliable partner may go bankrupt. Diversification of investments across several nations, geological prospects, and partners remains an important risk-management tool. A well-constructed portfolio should be resistant to the failure of any one nation, project, or relationship.

After all, there is no such thing as certainty. Reality can swiftly diverge from even the most careful of projections. In my conversations with business and political leaders, they have often pondered the role of fortune in their lives. Ideas they thought would be successful failed miserably, yet seemingly inferior ones soared to unanticipated heights. Perhaps the best answer is to have many horses in the contest of life; it's impossible to pick out the winners from the losers before the race is run.

CPSIA information can be obtained
at www.ICGtesting.com
Printed in the USA
LVOW10s0217161216
517531LV00002B/56/P

9 781466 439474